Clint

From one Motorola Teacher-Shrink to another

Best regards

Bob Feichtel

Motivator Teacher Shrink

How To Attract and Develop
Highly Successful Salespeople

BOB TEICHART

MOTES PUBLISHING
St. Charles, Illinois

Published by Motes Publishing
P.O. Box 1034
St. Charles, IL 60175

Cataloging-in-Publication Data

Teichart, Bob.
Motivator, teacher, shrink : how to attract and develop highly
successful salespeople / Bob Teichart.
St. Charles, IL : Motes Pub., 2007.
p. ; cm.
ISBN: 978-0-9797791-0-7
1. Sales personnel—Training of.
2. Sales personnel—Recruiting. I. Title.
HF5439.8.T45 2007
658.3/1245—dc22   2007904844

Book production and coordination
by Jenkins Group, Inc.
www.bookpublishing.com

Cover design by Chris Rhoads
Interior design by David Fideler

Printed in the United States of America
18 17 16 15 14 · 6 5 4 3 2

Dedication

This book is dedicated to:

My daughter, Alison,
who gave me a different viewpoint
on what coaching means.

and

My brother, Bruce.
I wish I knew then
what I know now.

Contents

Preface

My coaching career started in 1962, when I was still in high school. I was a sophomore and a member of the swim team at Hinsdale Central High School, in Hinsdale, Illinois. Sitting next to me was one of the best swimmers on the team. To my surprise, he started asking *me* to help him think through his race strategy for the events he was going to compete in that day.

I was just an average performer on the team, but that didn't matter to him. He was looking for advice to help him perform at his best, and he realized that I might have insights or ideas that would assist him. Today, I realize that anyone, regardless of ability, who wants to perform at his or her best, seeks advice from other people.

Since that experience more than forty years ago, I have participated on high-performing teams and have worked with world-class coaches in the fields of athletics and sales leadership. Through my coaching of both world-class athletes (including thirty-four High School All-Americans in the sport of swimming) and top performers in sales and sales leadership, I have gained insight into what is required for individuals to consistently perform at their best *and* to continue to improve.

Professionally, I am a product of four key relationships in my life. First, was Tony Canino, my high school freshman football coach. Tony was also my advisor during my years of teaching and coaching at Hinsdale Central High School. His drive to succeed was evident in the accomplishments of the teams and athletes he coached. Tony always challenged me to go after big goals, both as a teen and as an adult.

Next, is Don Watson. I was Don's assistant swim coach at Hinsdale Central High School, in Hinsdale, Illinois, for four years. Don's ability as a teacher and motivator gave me the foundation to achieve the success I have enjoyed since. While I was Don's assistant, he was coaching four swimmers who were world-record holders, two of whom were Olympic gold medal winners. My experience working with Don gave me the confidence and belief in myself to coach the best of the best, and I would not have succeeded as a swim coach without it.

The third influential person in my career is Donald D'Amico, EdD. Don was the superintendent of schools in St. Charles, Illinois, who took a risk and gave a twenty-nine-year-old teacher the chance to be the school district's first swim coach. Don taught me how to lead by example, and his belief and support helped me achieve the mutual goal of making St. Charles's swimming one of the top swim programs in the nation.

Finally, the fourth person who impacted my career is Charles Betts, MD, a psychiatrist from Little Rock, Arkansas, who helped me overcome my self-limiting thinking and enhance my coaching abilities. Since 1991, Charles has been *my* performance coach. He taught me how to be a better listener and to uncover the root causes of performance problems. This helped me to become a better resource to help my clients overcome the normal fears, doubts, and anxieties that impede progress, success, and continued growth. I would not be where I am personally or professionally without his assistance.

I wish I could say that I have been successful in helping everyone I have ever coached reach his or her goals, but I can't. The process of identifying the barriers to change, getting people to accept the responsibility to overcome them, and then helping them deal with the anxiety of implementing growth strategies is a complex, and at times frustrating, thing to do. Most importantly, the success of the process depends on the individual who is implementing it.

However, people can reach their goals, and as a sales coach, you have a powerful influence on whether that occurs. This book will provide you with an effective, practical framework to help you attract, retain, and motivate successful salespeople, and reach your own professional goals as well. In the chapters that follow, you'll learn how to:

1. Minimize the stress associated with influencing the behavior of the salespeople you lead;
2. Improve performance so both you and your salespeople achieve mutual goals; and
3. Retain your best people.

With a strategy in place, you'll find that motivating people and helping them change isn't as difficult as you may believe. While it has its challenges, I've found that the rewards for helping people improve the quality of their lives are worth the occasional frustration. I believe you will, too, and wish you and the people you lead continued success.

—BOB TEICHART

Acknowledgments

This book is a result of learning and working with a lot of people over a long period of time, starting with the athletic coaches I had: Bob Counsel, Tony Canino, Jay Kramer, Bill Trescott, Jerry Farmer, Dick Miller, and Harvey Dickinson; also, my speech teacher, Patte Maneese. Then, the coaches I worked for: John Weber, Don Watson, and Gene Strode.

My clients played a big part in writing this book because they challenged me to get better. One especially is John McDonnell, who I made a commitment to in January 2005, to get my ideas of coaching into print.

When I put the beginning draft together and Debbie Hill did the first editing, I realized I needed help to get a book published.

I am a much better speaker than a writer, so I dictated the content of this book. Willine Mahoney did the transcription. I don't know how she could listen to my recordings and type at the same time, but she did.

Kelly James-Enger is the writer I collaborated with to take the completed dictation and turn it into a concise and readable format. She challenged me to be better at doing what I do naturally, and turn my ideas into a transferable set of skills and insights. This book would not be as user-friendly had it not been for Kelly. What a pleasure it was working with her. Her professionalism and talent made a good book better.

Jerry Jenkins, the president of the Jenkins Group, was just the person to get this book published. His team of Nikki Stahl and Leah Nicholson arranged the design, layout, and publishing of the book. They were great to work with, and are very talented. Janice Karlovich did the editing and added many ideas that benefit the reader.

And lastly, to my wife, Dana, who had to give up our time together so I could spend time on this book project. Her patience and ability to put up with my frustrations is much appreciated. She was always available to assist me in meeting the requests of all the people who helped with the book project.

Introduction

The Coach's Playbook:
A Must for Sales Leaders

"The buck stops here."
President Harry S. Truman's famous and oft-cited quotation applies to you as well. As a sales leader, the buck stops with you. You're responsible for the success—or failure—of your team. That means that every member of your team plays an integral part in achieving the team's goals.

To achieve those goals, you've probably developed your own techniques for motivating your sales force, recruiting potential sales superstars, and prodding the people on your team to higher levels of achievement. In fact, one sales coach I know maintains a "technique book," which he's always updating with new "best practices" as he learns them at workshops.

Like this coach, you may have your own playbook—but are the techniques it includes still working? Does it need some new strategies? Or are you newer to the field and wish you had a proven method of recruiting and retaining successful sales people—and of helping them reach their highest potential?

Motivating yourself to achieve a goal is one thing. You know what drives you. You know what your dreams are, how hard you're willing to work, how much you can push yourself. Even with this self-knowledge, however, we often fall short of our expectations and fail to meet our own goals.

It's not surprising, then, that when it comes to motivating others; we also tend to fall short. We don't really understand the process. Complicating matters is that what works for us may not work for someone else—or worse yet,

1

it may actually inhibit that person's progress. That's why an effective sales coach uses more than his or her own experience to motivate others. An effective sales coach has strategies that have been proven to work with many people. Through time and trial by error, the coach knows what strategies to employ—and which to use if the first ones don't work. Those strategies make up the coach's playbook or technique book. Think of it as the system you use that provides direction to deal with the complexity of influencing human behavior.

Playbooks are developed over time, encompassing the ever-increasing knowledge of the coach, and can be adapted to specific situations as needed. When I do a workshop with sales coaches, I find that many already have playbooks—whether they call them that or not.

My goal isn't for them to toss out what's worked in the past. Rather it's to give them new ideas, new strategies, and new concepts that they can add to their system by selecting the concepts and techniques that they think will work for them. If you don't already have a playbook, you can use the information in this book to start developing one with these strategies as the foundation. Either way—whether you're starting a playbook or adding to one that already exists—you'll find the concepts, strategies, and techniques here that will enhance and improve your sales coaching skills.

My Personal Playbook

During my more than forty years of coaching experience, I've developed my own playbook that includes sales motivation strategies that have worked for everyone from novice salespeople to superstar sales performers. My technique book is based around one core strategy: the Growth-Rate Formula. The Growth-Rate Formula quantifies a person's ability to grow, regardless of experience, motivation, or knowledge. It also helps identify areas of weakness to target to increase growth-rate, and can be used by anyone pursuing higher levels of achievement.

My playbook is divided into the following sections:

- Application of the Growth-Rate Formula ("GRF");
- Motivational strategies to help people change;
- Strategies to hire and retain top sales performers;
- Strategies to teach focus;

- Strategies to enhance the coaching process; and
- Strategies to determine which coaching role to play in different situations.

In this book, each section of my playbook is addressed in its own chapter. As you read this book, you'll learn what the Growth-Rate Formula is and how to apply it. You'll learn how to encourage, inspire, and motivate change both in yourself and in the people who work with you. You'll discover how to distinguish between salespeople with the potential for greater success and those without it, and how to help them develop their own abilities to focus and reach their goals. You'll learn a proven coaching process to help you connect with the people you're coaching and understand more about the three primary roles you play as a sales coach—motivator, teacher and shrink.

Most importantly, you'll learn how to become a more effective, more powerful sales coach. A great coach doesn't force a player to do something. He works with the player to create drive, and his strategies may vary depending on the people he's coaching. The most famous coaches may be known for their winning records, but those wins come from their ability to challenge and motivate their teams.

My idea of challenge isn't to tell someone to do something, or threaten them with ultimatums or consequences. Rather, challenge is holding up a mirror to people and helping them acknowledge where they are and where they want to go. Challenge can only occur when the player respects the coach, and vice versa. It is a result of a relationship between the coach and the individual player.

That's also the case with sales coaches. Your relationship with the people you're coaching is critical, and this relationship should be as open and honest as possible. As you develop this relationship, you can help increase drive, teach the skills, knowledge, and behavioral talents they need to succeed, and help them create a new way of thinking.

A new way of thinking. Does that sound too ambitious? It's not, once you understand the concepts in my playbook and gain specific direction on how to apply them. A quick overview of the chapters that follow will introduce you to the concepts, techniques, and exercises I'll be using in the pages that follow. Consider this an overview of the information you'll learn, and an easy way to quickly reference relevant material in the book.

The Playbook Elements

The Growth-Rate Formula

Motivation is difficult to quantify. Think about it. How do you distinguish between "sort of" motivated, "somewhat" motivated, "very" motivated, and "extremely" motivated? Complicating matters is that motivation is highly individual; the things that motivate one person won't do anything for another.

That's where the Growth-Rate Formula ("GRF") is so helpful. I developed the GRF over years of coaching people in a variety of fields. The GRF provides both the salesperson and the coach with a quantifiable figure representing that person's ability to grow. The concept of the growth-rate formula is that continued growth is the result of drive and new learning minus the interference of self-defeating thinking that clutters the mind.

Here's the formula in its simplest form:

$$D + NL - 2(SDT) = \text{Growth Rate}$$

Drive ("D") creates the energy to learn new things (new learning, or "NL") while self-defeating thinking ("SDT") decreases the drive to make change or think bigger. By understanding this formula and teaching it to the people you coach, you share the responsibility for sales growth. If you can teach the person you're coaching the formula, you can teach that person the ability to self-diagnose areas of improvement and how to assume responsibility for continued sales growth.

In Chapter One, you'll learn more about this formula, how to apply it, and how to use it to work with salespeople. The formula embraces the fact that the most effective coaches have inquiring minds that allow them to explore these four critical questions with the salesperson:

1. What is the goal that will create the drive to make change?
2. What are the reasons this goal is so important?
3. What does the person have to learn to achieve the goal?
4. What is the self-defeating thinking that is preventing the person from "thinking bigger," or preventing the implementation of new learning?

Analyzing these four areas gives the coach a realistic idea of how quickly the new goal will be achieved, and helps the salesperson better understand the dynamics that impact change. After reading Chapter One, you'll know how to apply it both to yourself and to those with whom you work, and understand how the concept fits into the overall playbook.

The Secret of Change

For a highly motivated person, change can seem easy. You simply decide what you want, and go after it. But what happens when, as a sales coach, you're responsible not for changing yourself, but for helping others change? How do you motivate someone else? By challenging them—in a positive way.

It's simple to challenge others. In fact, it is rare to meet many people in positions of authority—parents, teachers, coaches or bosses—who fail to challenge the individuals they care about to be better. Challenge is the easy part. Effective, positive challenge that initiates a *change in behavior* is more difficult to master. An effective coach must know:

1. What must happen before you challenge others to change;
2. When and how strongly to challenge others;
3. Why you may challenge in a negative manner; and
4. How to gain the respect of the person you're challenging.

When you understand these four concepts, you can create a two-way dialogue that will enable you and the person you're challenging to develop a strategy to achieve the agreed-upon goal. In Chapter Two, you'll learn more about this process, and why respect is such an integral part of it. You'll also understand the difference between positive and negative challenge, and learn how to avoid doing the latter. The key concept to remember is that people change when they are constantly challenged by someone they respect.

Identifying and Attracting Talent

In some instances, you may lead people who you did not hire. But often, as a sales coach, you will have the opportunity to interview and select sales-people—to recruit the members of your team. How do you decide who to hire? While past performance is the best indicator of future results, the answer isn't limited to the individual's prior accomplishments. Rather, you look for a person who demonstrates three qualities—someone who is personable, coachable, and who wants to achieve exceptional goals.

Personable is easy enough. A personable person is someone you like, and it's an essential element of a potential candidate because it's virtually impossible to coach someone you don't care for. It's also relatively easy to determine someone who is highly goal-oriented. The second element—coachability—can be more difficult to assess.

Just as motivation is unique to every person, different people have varying levels of "coachability." It is nearly impossible to influence someone who doesn't want to be influenced; you also want to hire someone who you believe wants to achieve a common goal that benefits both of you. This is the essence of coachability.

You can determine coachability by:

1. Knowing what an ideal candidate looks like and which qualities are the most important to look for;
2. Structuring the selection process so that it establishes you as a leader;
3. Having a set of questions to identify who this candidate is and what he or she wants; and
4. Determining whether the candidate demonstrates behaviors that would make it difficult to work together.

In Chapter Three, you'll learn how to structure the interview and selection process to identify candidates who are coachable, and to weed out candidates who appear promising, but who would be difficult to coach. You'll also learn the importance of having a common goal among your team members, and how to establish that goal from the outset.

The Power of Focus

As kids, nearly all of us took a magnifying glass on a sunny day and focused the rays of the sun on a piece of paper. While the sun was hot, it wasn't hot enough on its own to burn the paper—until we increased the intensity of the sun's rays by focusing them with the magnifying glass.

One of your jobs as a coach is to help salespeople focus. To do so, you start by assessing and identifying the person's drive by using a "Focus Document." Then you develop major strategies to help the person achieve the goal that's creating the drive. Finally, you develop a specific "Breakthrough Learning Document" the salesperson will use to attain the major strategies and thus achieve the goal. In this way, you're drilling down from the macro to the micro with a target goal, major strategies to accomplish the goal, and the specific steps that will help you meet the major strategies.

In short, the process entails the following three steps:

1. Assisting the salesperson in identifying an unmet need that creates energy;
2. Identifying the new learning required to satisfy the unmet need; and
3. Implementing a tactical plan that accelerates learning.

Focus is an important concept for salespeople for another reason. There is a key concept in psychology that says the mind goes into overload when it has more than three things to focus on. Too many options, and it's too difficult to focus your energy. Other coaches mean the same thing when they use the phrase "Keep it simple, stupid," or "KISS."

In Chapter Four, you'll learn how individuals can make significant change when they focus on these breakthrough strategies, and why the coach's job is to help them create and focus their energy. You'll also learn how to use the Focus Document and Breakthrough Learning Document as you work with salespeople.

The Coaching Process

Just because the salesperson has a focus and the tactical plan to achieve the goal doesn't mean the coach's job is over. Implementing anything new creates anxiety. It feels awkward writing one's name with the opposite hand. Magnify this anxiety ten-fold when a person is trying to implement new skills, knowledge, habits, and ways of thinking. It's not surprising that, all too often, anxiety prevents the person from successfully implementing change.

A good coach helps people understand the negative feelings and thinking they experience when they change. The most effective coaches go further and help them minimize the negative or anxious energy these feelings and thoughts generate. The coach's role at this stage is multifaceted. As a coach, you should:

1. Teach people what anxiety really is;
2. Clarify the difference between the performance self and the emotional self;
3. Create a safe environment where the internal conflicts that prevent

change can be discussed and resolved;

4. Be open to being challenged on how well you're performing as a coach;
5. Have an appropriate coaching agenda;
6. Assist the person in dealing with the normal defenses that are encountered when he or she is asked to make a change; and
7. Have the data that indicates the amount of progress (a "reality check") that is being made.

As a coach, you build relationships by helping people deal with the inherent anxiety surrounding change, and successfully alter their thoughts, behaviors, and habits. In Chapter Five, you'll learn more about effectively coaching people through the process of change.

Motivator, Teacher, Shrink

Ever wanted to simply tell someone, "Just do what I say, and you will be successful"? After all, as a sales leader, you already know from first-hand experience the skills, habits, and thinking of top salespeople. The problem is that the people you coach don't always do what you tell them!

The role you're expected to play as coach depends on the specific situation the person you're coaching is facing. You may have to help motivate him or her to reach a goal. You might have to teach the person how to do something. Or you may have to diagnose why someone is struggling with anxiety as he attempts to change. That's where your three roles—motivator, teacher, shrink—come in.

In Chapter Six, you'll learn how to accelerate change by using the three roles of a coach. You'll learn how to:

1. Continue to apply the GRF concept described in detail in Chapter One to diagnose the root cause for lack of performance;
2. Motivate someone, and what type of discussion to have when someone's drive to learn isn't there;
3. Implement an improved learning model; and
4. Use exercises to minimize the normal resistance to change.

It's often easy to diagnose a problem. Determining the appropriate prescription can be more difficult. This final chapter will provide insight into the ongoing coaching process and help you determine which role is most effective for you to use at different times. As you master these roles, you'll become more effective at motivating others to change while helping them to meet their individual goals.

1

The Growth-Rate Formula

Key concept: Continued growth is the result of drive and new learning minus the interference of self-defeating thinking that clutters the mind.

I magine this. You're sitting at your desk, studying the quarterly sales figures for your team. Today you'll be meeting with several team members—one of your top performers, another who meets her sales goals but rarely exceeds them, and a newer salesperson who hasn't met his sales targets for the past two quarters.

Who has the greatest potential out of these three salespeople? You might be tempted to say the first one—the top performer who's proven himself. But the other two salespeople—the "average" performer and the one who's falling short—may have greater potential to grow than their apparent better.

It's nearly impossible to measure potential based on sales figures alone. An experienced sales coach may "go by his gut," and rely on instinct when evaluating potential. But I've found that quantifying potential growth in a formula—the Growth-Rate Formula, or GRF—gives a specific number to assess potential growth. The GRF also lets you assess drive, the amount of new learning necessary for the person to achieve a specific goal, and the degree to which the salesperson is held back by internal factors.

But the GRF goes beyond that. It also allows the sales coach to diagnosis the root of a performance problem and makes for better two-way communication when the salesperson assesses his or her own performance using the formula.

While few sales managers use a specific formula like the GRF to diagnose the root cause of a performance problem or to assess potential growth, its application can make a significant difference in not only your team's sales numbers, but in your rapport with your salespeople as well. Using the formula—and teaching it to the people you coach—creates a shared responsibility for sales growth. It also lets salespeople self-diagnose areas of potential improvement, regardless of their experience levels.

The GRF, broken down to a mathematical formula, consists of:

$$D + NL - 2(SDT) = \text{Growth Rate}$$

These three elements include Drive ("D"), or the desire to achieve a goal. Drive, in turn, creates the energy to learn new things, defined as New Learning, or "NL." Both of these factors increase rate of growth, but Self-Defeating Thinking ("SDT") decreases the drive to make change significantly—by about a factor of two. Princeton University professor Daniel Kahneman, Ph.D., won the Nobel Prize in economics in 2002 for his research examining human psychology's impact on economic decisions. Kahneman has found that people avoid risk twice as much as they seek opportunity for gain. In the GRF, these risks are represented by Self-Defeating Thinking.

Drive: The Motivating Factor

We're all familiar with the concept of drive, but what exactly does this term mean? Drive can be defined as the amount of energy directed toward achieving a meaningful goal.

One classic example of drive is the successful mission to the moon. On May 25, 1961, President John F. Kennedy announced his intention for the U.S. to put a man on the moon and to return safely by the end of the decade. This goal—which would have been unthinkable just a decade before—created a tremendous amount of drive. Our national pride was at stake! The fear that the Russians, who were developing their own space program, might get there before us was another motivating factor—our country's security must be protected. All of these factors created tremendous drive to move forward to meet the goal of putting a man on the moon.

Keep in mind that drive must start with a *goal*. Without a goal to achieve, there is no drive. The goals that inspire and motivate salespeople vary from person to person. Working with the salesperson to select goals that complement the person's inner needs is the key, but to do this you must understand the salesperson's needs. In some cases, the needs will be apparent, but in others, you may have to question the person to get a greater understanding of what's truly motivating him or her.

I've found that the five primary needs for salespeople are: impact, recognition, money, mastery, and sense of belonging. Let's look at each of these in turn:

Impact

A salesperson that cares about impact might use the phrase, "I want to do something that really makes a difference." Impact is an evangelistic zeal. It's a sense of believing that what you do makes a difference in people's lives, and a sense of fulfillment in making that difference.

How can you tell if a salesperson is motivated by making an impact? Listen for phrases like: "I believe clients and prospects need someone like me to assist them in solving their problems and achieving their goals," or "I want to help more people."

Think of the old story about the person who comes upon three masons laying brick for a building. When asked what they are doing, the first mason says, "I'm laying brick."

The second mason's reply is different. He says, "I'm making $30/hour so I can provide for my family."

The third mason says, "I'm part of the team that's building one of the most beautiful churches in the area where families will gather to enjoy worship together." It's this person who is motivated by the ability to make an impact. In short, impact is a personal sense of purpose and a belief that "What I do makes a difference."

Recognition

Recognition is the desire to be known—in this case, for doing outstanding work. In other words, the salesperson wants to consistently be performing at the top of his or her peer group to receive that kind of acknowledgment.

A person who is motivated by recognition may mention awards won in the past, or always be focused on winning yet another sales award. This is a person who thrives on, even feeds on, praise for doing outstanding work. He or she is delighted to be written up in the company newsletter or acknowledged in other ways for work accomplishments. This salesperson needs recognition and will do whatever it takes to get it.

Understand that the recognition the person seeks may be limited to a specific field or area of achievement. I learned this firsthand—when I was a high school teacher and swim coach, I spent long days both in the classroom and at the pool. People would tell me, "If you put this much time into a career in the financial services industry, you'd make a lot more money." But that wasn't the point. I wasn't interested in making a lot more money. I was more interested in winning swim meets and being recognized by the top performers in my peer group—in this case, extremely successful coaches. Today, while I've changed fields, one of my primary needs remains the same—to be recognized.

Money

First, let's do away with the stereotypical money-obsessed, greedy salesperson. This isn't what I'm talking about when I refer to someone who's motivated by money. Rather, someone who is motivated by money believes that "money can give my family and me a much better quality of life." This is a powerful belief. People with a need to make large amounts of income may also want to help organizations they care about, provide a high-quality education for their children, and create a sense of stability for the people they love.

In addition, money provides a benchmark and lets you compare your income to that of your peers in the industry. If you're making a lot of money, your financial success announces that you're a leader in your career. In fact, in most professions, money is a byproduct of high achievement—if you're really good at what you do, the money will be there.

In the field of sales, money is a concrete form of recognition. You might want to be recognized for your intellectual capital, but that won't happen—unless you make enough sales. Then you're recognized for making those stellar sale figures (which probably did occur because of your knowledge base) by making more money.

From a capitalistic standpoint, money drives the economy and creates more jobs. People who make money spend money, and create new opportunities for others that didn't exist before. While most salespeople are motivated by money to some degree, some find it their primary motivation. Someone who didn't come from money and had to work very hard to become successful may see money as the most important benchmark, recognizing the opportunities it provides.

In short, money-motivated salespeople who are successful are not the greedy people some might think. They do want to have fun, and enjoy their "toys." They also want their family to have nice things, and they are generous in giving money to organizations they care about. They also are willing to spend money on learning and expanding their businesses. Finally, they don't need to brag about how successful they are because they are having fun. They are capitalists at heart—i.e., they know that money drives the economy, and they look at money as a tool, not as inherently bad, or the root cause of evil.

Mastery

A person who is motivated by mastery might say, "I want to be exceptional in all areas of my profession," or "I want to be a world-class salesperson."

When I think of mastery, I think of Tiger Woods. Tiger Woods certainly doesn't need any more money. He doesn't need any more recognition. It might be nice, but it's not what drives him. Rather, he wants to master his career and every aspect of it—and as a result, more rewards will follow.

Salespeople who are driven by mastery want to excel at every aspect of their careers as well. They're not satisfied to do one thing well—once they've acquired a new skill, whether it's developing new leads or learning more about the products they offer, they're seeking the next challenge. They understand that their business is constantly changing, and embrace the challenge of staying on top of it.

If you have a salesperson who says, "I want to be the best that I can be," that suggests that a desire for mastery is present. This person may also seek out new activities—from skydiving to scuba diving to sailing—and thrive on constantly challenging himself or herself to become better. Again, mastery is the driving factor.

Sense of Belonging

Don't overestimate the desire to be part of not just a group, but part of *the* group. A person who's driven by a sense of belonging might say, "I want to be part of a group that is working together to achieve an exciting common goal."

According to evolutionary psychologists, only about ten percent of the population truly has a vision for the future. The other ninety percent are looking for someone with a vision so they can join the group. In other words, the majority of people aren't seeking to lead or change the future. We just want to be a member of someone's team who does want to lead. The peer pressure of belonging to a group and performing as an integral member of that group can be a powerful motivator.

Consider the several million Americans who enlisted in the military immediately after the attack on Pearl Harbor. In fact, out of the sixteen million Americans who served in the military throughout World War II, more than half—nine million—of them voluntarily risked their lives for their country. These men and women of the "Greatest Generation" wanted to belong to a cause that was important. They didn't think twice about joining the military—rather, they said, "This is important and we need to get it done." We saw a similar reaction, albeit on a smaller scale, after the events of September 11, 2001, where people who had never previously considered military service enlisted.

The astronauts and NASA employees who worked for years to advance the moon mission had a similar dedication. The person who's motivated by a sense of belonging thrives on being part of a team. Salespeople with this need talk about the team over the individual, focusing on the group's efforts and achievements over their own.

In fact, the power of belonging to a group can spur individuals on to greater accomplishments. Several years ago, I traveled to the Pecos River Ranch near Santa Fe, New Mexico, as part of a team-building exercise with some of my clients. One morning, our group of thirty went out to the top of a high bluff. There, each of us hooked our carabiner, or safety clip, to the steel cable suspended above the river 400 feet below—and literally jumped off the cliff to cross to the other side. Like many people, I had always been nervous around heights. But I jumped. In fact, twenty-nine of us did.

That night, during a debriefing exercise, we were asked how many of us would have jumped had we been alone at the top. Only two said they would have jumped had they been by themselves. I saw firsthand how the need to belong and to receive approval from a group could cause people to confront their fears. In other words, simply being a member of a team can help people overcome self-defeating thinking and achieve their goals.

Assessing Drive

When you're working with a salesperson, consider the amount of drive the person demonstrates. Is the person's work ethic focused on learning and doing? Does she arrive at work early and stay late—and make the most of her work day? Is she eager to tackle new responsibilities? Does she have energy? Is she focused on her goals, not allowing distractions to take her off-course? Is she a risk taker? Does she know how to prioritize? Does she make quick decisions and communicate directly? These are all examples of drive. People who have drive are disciplined and follow through on commitments, even when they're tired, discouraged, or simply having a bad day.

If you don't see significant drive, it's your responsibility as sales coach to assist the salesperson in identifying which needs are still unmet—and then establishing a goal that satisfies those needs. This will create the drive to improve sales results. An extreme example of drive is the drug addict—he will do whatever it takes to get his next fix. While you don't want salespeople to embrace such a literally life-threatening drive, your job is to help determine what specific unmet needs will create high drive in your salespeople.

Keep in mind, too, that you want to help teach your salespeople how to figure out what's important to them, and to get a better handle on their own unmet needs. That's how they can understand why a particular goal is important to them, figure out what they need to learn to be able to achieve it, and identify the self-defeating thinking that's holding them back. If, as a sales coach, you can teach the people you're working with to do that for themselves, they can begin to take responsibility for maintaining their own drive.

In fact, sustaining drive or motivation is often the most difficult task for a successful salesperson who has already reached most of his goals. Neil Armstrong, the first man on the moon, struggled with this same issue. He achieved something amazing and remarkable, and became a household name. But imagine how it felt to be him after that momentous occasion. "I am the first person to set foot on the moon. What can I do that will ever top this accomplishment?" In other words, what's next?

Armstrong says that he struggled for several years after the successful moon mission to determine what was next—to find something that was important to him that would give him the same sense of fulfillment he had working to become an astronaut. While salespeople may not go to the moon in the literal sense, the feeling of "nothing left to achieve" strikes many successful ones mid- to late-career. Figuring out an unmeet need—one that will create drive—is the answer. Just keep in mind that if an extraordinarily driven person like Neil Armstrong can struggle with lack of drive, so can everyone else.

As a sales coach, you don't want to make the mistake of setting a goal that *you* want your salesperson to achieve. Rather, you want to set a goal that you *both* want the person to achieve. Motivation must be internal for it to be self-sustaining, so you want to explore the five primary need factors discussed above to help determine what goal would be appropriate. We'll talk more about motivating your sales team in Chapter Six.

New Learning: What Must Happen Next?

Once you have identified the current drive level of the salesperson, the next step is to assess whether the salesperson has the skills, knowledge, and habits necessary to make progress in his career. This is relatively easy. An experienced sales coach can observe the skills, knowledge, and habits of the top salespeople to see how they compare to the salesperson you are working with.

Regardless of how much drive or how little self-defeating thinking an individual has, if he doesn't know how to do something, he will fail. Let's look at an example. Bill is a world-record holder in swimming. He's never skied before, however, and his friend Joe invites him to Colorado to ski. Joe happens to be a world-class skier, and he challenges his competitive buddy to go down the double diamond ski slope, the most difficult rating.

Anybody who's skied before understands that a novice on a double diamond (the most challenging) run could really injure—if not kill—himself because of the lack of skill. So even though Bill is a world-class swimmer, this absence of skill in a certain area—skiing—is devastating. For Bill's sake, let's hope he recognizes his lack of skill and starts out with some lessons on the bunny hill to determine his capabilities before he hits the powder with his buddy.

Let's look at another example in a sales setting. Pete isn't afraid to call anybody. He is driven to be the best, but he hasn't sold the new product before and it has sophisticated applications. Because of his lack of product knowledge—a lack of new learning—on how to sell this product, Pete won't be successful. If he educates himself about the product and its applications, however, he increases his chance for success.

Selling may appear to be a simple process between two people, but it's often a more complicated, involved interaction. First, you have the complexity of the product, which varies, and the knowledge of the product that goes with it. Depending on the product, the sales cycle can take weeks or months because of the number of steps (and decision-makers) involved. In some sales situations, you're only selling to one person. In others, there are a number of people involved in the process, which in turn increases the complexity. Finally, the level of knowledge that the potential buyers want their salesperson to have may be incredibly detailed and diverse—another level of complexity.

In complex selling situations like these, learning is the critical factor. No matter how hard you work—no matter how many calls you make, or how many new clients you develop—the key is "working smart." Six- and seven-figure salespeople must work smart, and be smart, because they must understand the uses of the product like an engineer, communicate and develop relationships like a psychologist, organize their administrative work like an efficiency expert, develop relationships with potential buyers like a public relations firm, and communicate a return on investment to prospects like a chief financial officer. That's a tremendous amount of learning that's necessary to succeed.

Another factor that affects the complexity of the sale is what type of sales situation the seller is facing. The first is a transactional sale, where the buyer just wants something quick and cheap. This *is* a relatively simple sale. The second type is the value-added sale. Here, the salesperson must demonstrate her knowledge of the applications of the product to show that it will meet the uses the buyer is seeking. Finally, the third type is a partnership sale. In this situation, the buyer wouldn't consider making the decision to buy the product without contacting the salesperson—in other words, having a relationship, or partnership, with her.

Note that as you move along that sales progression—transaction, value-added, and partnership—that the average income of the salesperson goes up. As a sales manager, you know that income for any salesperson is in direct proportion to the complexity of the sale, the length of the sales cycle, and the size of the problem that this sale is going to solve. As you consider all the elements that are included in the selling process, you can understand how much new learning a salesperson may need to continue to advance in her career.

And what exactly do salespeople need to learn? The new learning falls into these nine key areas:

1. *Product knowledge.* Remember Pete? All his effective selling techniques don't mean anything if he's not up to speed on what his product actually does, and how it can benefit potential customers. The amount of product knowledge a salesperson needs to learn may depend on the complexity of the product, his background with the product, and whether it's new or an updated version of a prior product.

2. *Selling skills.* What do you say when you contact a client for the first time? How do you close a sale? How much information do you provide to a prospect? What's the difference between assertive and aggressive selling—and which is the right fit for the situation? While it's true that some people are "born to sell," all salespeople need to develop selling techniques and strategies.

3. *Marketing systems to identify, obtain, and retain good clients.* Salespeople

must have systems in place that let them track potential, current, and past clients for more efficient, effective selling. The type of system may vary from person to person, but maintaining information about clients, as well as tracking contact with them is essential.

4. *Operational systems and staff to perform administrative tasks.* The most effective salespeople don't try to do everything themselves. They realize that support staff save them time and energy, freeing them up to focus on selling, rather than paperwork. But a salesperson who has never worked with support staff must learn how to manage people effectively, make the most of the systems already in place, and possibly even develop better ones.

5. *Understanding and using technology.* Today, it's easier for salespeople to work from the road, but not all of them are harnessing technology to the extent necessary to get their work done more quickly. Today, learning to use proposal and quoting software, client relationship management software, and marketing database programs is all part of a salesperson's job.

6. *Cross-selling.* Smart salespeople know that it's almost as easy to sell two products as it is to sell one—if you know how to do it. Cross-selling techniques, and an understanding of all of the products in your company, are essential knowledge for the most successful salespeople.

7. *Working with other members of one's organization to close large sales—in other words, being a team player.* All salespeople need an understanding of their company's hierarchy and the process of closing sales, as well as knowledge about the other "key players" at the organization—and the ability to act as a member of a team.

8. *Developing key relationships both inside and outside of the client's organization.* Particularly with complex sales, salespeople must develop and maintain relationships with a number of different people at the customer's company. The ability to do that—and a savvy knowledge of office politics—is critical for success, as is having connections with people outside the organization that may affect current and future sales.

9. *Using key measurements that create an effective way to track progress and success.* Salespeople are always looking for benchmarks, and the most effective realize that true growth may not be measured simply in total sales or in gross earnings. Salespeople may need to develop

new methods or standards to evaluate both their own and their team's progress, as well as finding and communicating data to prospects about their product's value and return on investment.

The fact is that salespeople are constantly learning in their careers, whether they're consciously striving to or not. The old saying, "People change but seldom," is false. Just think of what people have learned since they were in kindergarten! People do learn, even if it is at different rates. As a sales coach, remember that adults are most motivated to learn when that knowledge can immediately be used for something that they need. Successful coaches must be able to evaluate a salesperson's abilities, tell him what he needs to learn to achieve his goals, and highlight the connection between the learning and the goal.

Self-Defeating Thinking: A Powerful Player

Once you've determined a salesperson's drive and the amount and type of new learning that must occur, you must examine their self-defeating thinking. This aspect of diagnosing the cause of a performance problem can be as difficult as creating drive. That element is the self-defeating thinking that prevents the salesperson from thinking bigger, implementing his new learning, or both.

What is this self-defeating thinking that clutters the mind? It varies from person to person, but basically it's the thoughts and feelings people have when they start experiencing the normal anxiety that accompanies change. In a sales setting, it's the negative thinking that occurs when a salesperson attempts to set higher goals or learn new skills that will help her succeed.

Remember that salespeople need a strong and compelling reason (or more than one) to achieve a goal. That reason creates drive. The problem is that as human beings, even though we may be driven, we all want to stay comfortable, too. In other words, we want to hang out in our comfort zone. It feels good there, after all!

Self-defeating thinking kicks in when you start learning new things and moving in the direction of your goals. That movement creates discomfort because you're moving outside your comfort zone. Discomfort is a negative feeling, and negative feelings create negative thinking.

Keep in mind that experiencing these negative feelings doesn't mean you're weak or inept. Feelings—emotions—are always automatic. They're a survival mechanism. A hundred thousand years ago, those feelings—something as slight as a sense of uneasiness—protected our ancestors from harm. Then, edginess or vague discomfort could literally mean a threat to their lives.

Even today, we're hard-wired the same way. So when we experience something that feels uncomfortable, those feelings of anxiety and fear automatically kick in. They're not a sign of weakness. Rather, I encourage you to consider anxiety as a lack of mastery, not personal inadequacy. When you communicate that idea to the people you coach, you'll find them more willing to share their self-defeating thinking with you and you can work together to overcome it.

There are three basic areas of self-defeating thinking to examine with the people you coach:

Self-Concept

This is how one views himself. Does he see himself achieving the unmet need by achieving the goal? Can he envision himself implementing the new learning? All of us have experienced a situation where we wonder if we will fit in with our chosen group, or whether we're good enough to succeed. When I first went into business for myself, one of the first people I called on was very successful and he introduced me to other successful people. But when I was with them, my self-talk was largely negative. I remember thinking, "I'm never going to be as successful as these people." I just didn't see myself doing it.

Well, if you don't see yourself doing something, why would you even want to try? That's the problem with a negative self-concept. However, self-concept changes over time and can be improved. By going back and looking at the successes you've had and realizing that you can get better, you can also improve your self-concept. (On the other hand, you can focus only on your failures and make your self-concept even worse, but we're taking a positive spin here.) In short, your self-concept, at the most basic level, is your belief in yourself—in your abilities to achieve your goals and to succeed at new challenges.

Beliefs

Here, I mean beliefs not in one's self, but in the products you are selling and the techniques you use to do so. Does the salesperson believe in his products? Does he trust in the strategy that will get him to where he wants to go? Does he have faith that what he does makes a difference in the lives of his clients? If the answers to these questions are no, these beliefs will contribute to self-defeating thinking.

Salespeople also have beliefs about their potential customers and about the market potential for their products. These can be positive or negative. Think about it. A salesperson may think, "My products aren't as good as those of my competitors.'" Or, "My products are way better than my competitors'!" Perhaps there's a new option available and the salesperson is concerned this will cut into her market. Or the salesperson believes that her territory is a lousy one, or that her clients are notoriously slow to close, or that her boss isn't on her side and won't help her meet her goals. These are the kinds of beliefs—whether or not they are true—that impact self-defeating thinking.

Fear

There are many things to fear, but the most common fear for a salesperson is the worry that she can't handle the situation she's asking herself to face. As her fear grows, she'll start asking herself questions like, "What if I look foolish?" and "What will others think as I do this?" Nobody wants to look stupid. That's probably the reason why the number one fear of Americans isn't death, but public speaking.

Fear also includes the apprehension of loss. All change has an element of loss associated with it, because if the salesperson makes a change and it doesn't work out, she might lose money, status, or relationships. Someone fearing loss might ask herself questions like the following:

1. What if I spend money to get better results and I am unsuccessful?
2. Will my clients think as highly of me if I start working with product experts?
3. Will I lose friends if I start selling to them?

In short, the biggest fear for a salesperson is the inability to perform in a certain situation. Many salespeople are held back by the worry that they'll lose something—whether it's friends, or income, or simply respect. Understanding these fears and helping people overcome them is essential to reducing or deflecting self-defeating thinking.

Explain what self-defeating thinking is. Tell salespeople it's a normal response when they try something new. This helps open the lines of communication and lets you work with the person to evaluate the sources of self-defeating thinking. It's also important that salespeople understand the degree of impact that self-defeating thinking can have on their progress toward their goals. In essence, it has about twice the impact of drive.

Putting It into Practice

Recall the formula for diagnosing a person's ability to grow, the GRF:

$$D + NL - 2(SDT) = \text{Growth Rate}$$

(See the facing page for a graphic representation of the GRF.)

Why use the formula to diagnose performance problems? Here's the reason: As a sales coach, when you sit down with people and ask them why they're not as successful as they could be, they often start talking about gross generalities. (Or they start making excuses for their performance, which we'll discuss further in Chapters Four and Five.)

The way you help them move past the generalities and drill down to get specific is to ask where they see themselves in these three areas—drive, new learning, and self-defeating thinking. Ask them, "On a scale of 1 to 10, how driven are you? On a scale of 1 to 10, how much do you think you need to learn? On a scale of 1 to 10, how fearful are you about changing?" By having these numbers and calculating the person's GRF, we have a specific reference point to work with. As the person's coach, I also know that if the GRF is a lower number, we'll probably have to go slow. On the other hand, if your GRF is high, I can challenge you a lot more and put more demands on you. As a coach, you don't want to put someone into an overload situation, and you don't want to fail to challenge him either.

So, let's say you sit down with a person who's not performing well. You ask why, and the salesperson says, "I'm not in sync with my goals," or something equally vague. That's a general answer that doesn't help you analyze the problem. On the other hand, if you start talking about drive, and you ask the person to evaluate his drive and he says that it's a 10, you have a reference point—even if, as his sales coach, you estimate his drive as a 2. The number assigned to each element—drive, new learning, and self-defeating thinking—can be discussed individually, along with the person's overall GRF.

Now let's take a look at some examples of applying the formula.

You're working with a mid-career salesperson we'll call Janette. As Janette examines her current drive level compared to the time she was most driven in her career, she gives herself a score of 6, with 1 being no drive and 10 being maximum drive. Next, she looks at how much she needs to learn to achieve

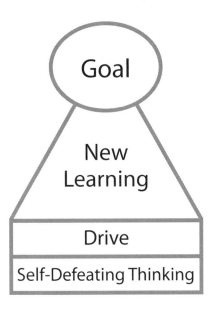

As you look at the diagram, keep these questions in mind:

- What is the *Goal*?
- What are the reasons that the goal is so important? (*Drive*)
- What *New Learning* is needed to achieve the goal?
- What is the *Self-Defeating Thinking* that is getting in the way of implementing the new learning or thinking bigger?

Figure 1.1: Growth-Rate Formula

the goals that are important to her. She knows individuals who are already where she wants to be in the future and gives them a learning level of 10.

Janette assesses her progress and realizes she is about half way to knowing what they know, so she gives herself a score of 5 on a scale of 1 to 10. Finally, she has some self-defeating thinking that creates anxiety as she thinks about committing to the goal and starting to learn new things, so she gives herself a score of 4. A rating of 1 means almost no self-defeating thinking (there's always some level of self-defeating thinking, whether we realize it or not) while a 10 would mean severe self-defeating thinking.

Doing the math, her growth rate result is 6 + 5—2(4) = 3. This score is out of a maximum score of 18. Think about it—the highest drive possible is 10, and if the person has nothing to learn, an NL score of 10. That's 20, but you still have to deduct 2, or 2(1) to represent the subconscious self-defeating thinking we're unaware of. So, 10 + 10—2 = 18 is the maximum growth rate possible. (For a more detailed exercise for salespeople to use to determine their growth rate, see the Appendix, page 126.)

From assessing her GRF, Janette now knows that to increase the growth rate she will have to:

1. Identify an unmet need that will increase her drive.
2. Start learning new things that will improve performance.
3. Figure out how to minimize her self-defeating thinking.

As Janette's sales coach, it's your job to be a resource to help her do those three things. The GRF tells you and Janette—or any other salesperson you're working with—whether growth will be slow or fast and takes the mystery out of why performance isn't better. The higher the GRF, the quicker the person will reach her goal.

One of the advantages of the GRF is that you can use it with both new and seasoned salespeople. Following are several real-life examples of applying the GRF:

The New Salesperson

Justin is brand new to the world of sales. He was a former customer of the firm that he just started to work for. Justin decided to try sales, as he wanted to improve the quality of his life and thought that he could make more money in sales.

Justin is a natural extrovert who has always enjoyed helping people and now wants to be rewarded for it. While he hasn't had any sales-specific training, he has tremendous intellectual capital around the products that he's going to sell because he used them professionally before launching his sales career.

Sitting down with Justin and going through the GRF, it's clear he has a definite goal in mind. He wants to double the income that he was making in his previous job, and he has tremendous drive to do so. At his former job, he made a fixed salary; here, he has the opportunity to make commissions and can either make more, or less, than he did before.

You're working with Justin and have identified the goal—to produce more income than he did last year. Justin says his drive level is 8—after all, he's got to pay his bills. You look at how much he needs to learn and he's about a 6 on new learning. Not surprisingly, all of the new learning is about how to sell. Justin has to learn how to build trusting relationships, to uncover problems customers want to solve, and to develop and present solutions to those problems. He also has to learn how to handle objections (such as price) from clients that prevent implementation of the solutions, and to perform the follow-through necessary to implement the solution—in short, how to close. His firsthand product knowledge is stellar, but he still lacks a basic understanding of how to sell to people.

When you examine self-defeating thinking, you find Justin has some issues here as well. While he wants the income, he has never really seen himself as a salesperson. In fact, he hasn't really liked salespeople. He has a belief in the product that he's going to be selling, so that is not a problem, but he has a lot of fears. What if he doesn't succeed? He'll have the embarrassment, even shame, at not being successful because he had a successful track record where he was before. So, when you look at self-defeating thinking, you have a 5 for Justin.

Justin's GRF

$$8 + 6 - 2(5) = 4$$

A rate of growth of 4 means that it's going to take him a little while to get up to the income level he's seeking. But the biggest opportunity here is that now you can direct him to your organization's training program to learn the selling skills as quickly as possible. As his sales coach, you can also explore his self-concept about being in sales and help prevent his fears from getting in his way, especially when he encounters rejection.

The Talented So-So Performer

Alex has been with your company for five years. You'd describe him as a slightly above-average performer. He likes what he does; he's personable and friendly and people in the company like him. More importantly, customers really like him.

But as we go through the GRF with Alex, we discover that he doesn't have a significant goal. One of the reasons is his self-concept. He's never seen himself as a top producer, and he's also fearful of going in another direction because he doesn't want to break relationships with his current clients. Alex has been asked to start looking at a new market, but his relationships with his clients are extremely important to him. While he receives tremendous recognition from clients, he doesn't capitalize on this opportunity to move forward and, as a result, has not had some of the results that other salespeople have had. Alex does demonstrate the sales skills that are necessary to succeed—in fact, he could actually teach the class on "how to sell" and mentors some of the newer salespeople.

You'd like Alex to continue to grow and improve, but one of the problems is his lack of a clear goal. He has a sales figure he's supposed to meet each year, but because it's not really *his* goal, he resists it. He wonders whether it's a realistic goal and every year doubts whether he'll be able to meet it. (Again, this is self-defeating thinking.) From a drive level, without a definite goal that he's motivated by, Alex is about a 5. No one can question his skill—in fact, people say, "That Alex is so talented—why hasn't he been successful?" So you give him a 10 for new learning.

It's the self-defeating thinking that's holding him back. Alex doesn't see himself as a top salesperson (self-concept). He believes he must be extremely helpful to the clients he has (beliefs) and he is afraid to risk building new markets because he'll lose clients or lose status by losing income (fear.) So, for self-defeating thinking, he's a 7.

Alex's GRF
$$5 + 10 - 2(7) = 1$$

Now you can see that even with his stellar sales skills, it will take significant time for Alex to develop and reach greater sales goals. But at least you've diagnosed the problem and can help him overcome it.

The Sales Star

Your final producer is Kim. Kim has been with the company and has been one of the top salespeople in this company for as long as you can remember. She's had some opportunities presented to her because the company wants her to assume responsibility for a special project that could give her tremendous income potential. However, she has resisted it. Kim is happy. She's satisfied with where she's at. So even though she is a top producer and has a tremendous knowledge level of what to do and how to succeed, the drive to make a change just isn't there.

Thinking about a goal that would take her in another direction just isn't relevant. She'll resist it, thinking, "I'm happy, so why would I want to change? I was told I'd have a tremendous lifestyle if I succeeded as a salesperson, and I've got it. I like the money I make. I like the house I live in. I like the recognition I get."

Knowing all this as her sales coach, you see a person who's not sure of a goal other than to maintain exactly where she is at. So let's assess her drive at about a 3. From the new learning perspective, she knows everything she needs to know about how to be successful—in other words, a 10.

Her self-concept is also very strong. Kim sees herself as being at the top, and she's there. The new assignment that she is being asked to assume is of little interest to her. She doesn't see herself as being somebody who would take on a project like that. She doesn't believe she needs to make a change. And the fear of putting a successful career at risk is overwhelming, giving a total self-defeating score of 7.

Kim's GRF

$$3 + 10 - 2(7) = -1$$

That's a GRF of -1—for the top producer at your company! Now you understand why she won't be motivated to take on this new responsibility, or why it will take her a long time to be convinced.

As you can see from these real-life examples, using the GRF and talking about it with your salespeople gives you insight into what they're thinking and feeling, and what their aspirations are for the future. This will help give you, as the sales coach, a sense of direction as to what role to play. With Justin, your new salesperson, motivation is not the issue. Your job is to provide some learning and help him with his self-concept and fear issues. Your so-so producer Alex needs no learning at all, but you can help him discover what would motivate him to change and how to overcome the fears and anxiety that the change will instigate. For your top producer Kim, you'll have to figure out something that will be exciting for her and help her see that her fears and beliefs and self-concept issues might be irrational. You'll learn more about these three primary sales coach roles—motivator, teacher, and shrink—in Chapter Six.

2

The Secret of Change

Key concept: People change when they receive constant challenge from someone they respect.

As a sales coach, one of your primary functions is to motivate your team. Knowing what drives each individual salesperson is the first step to doing so, as it gives you the information you need to work with each of them to set goals. Calculating the person's GRF will tell you how fast to expect the person to change, and how high to set the bar in terms of performance. All too often, however, sales coaches overlook a critical element of motivating people to change—that the challenge must come from someone the salesperson respects.

Remember that the sales coaching relationship is a two-way street. You can't simply tell your team members what to do, or what their goals are. You work together to determine goals and which strategies to use to accomplish them. Whether you realize it or not, your sales team members look to you for encouragement, advice, and more importantly, modeling. In other words, you have to "walk the talk." You're a role model for everyone on your team, and if they deem you worthy of respect, they'll be willing to work with you to change. If they don't respect you, however, you'll find it difficult to motivate them—and you may never understand the reason why!

Gaining Respect

You start building a relationship with someone from the moment you meet him or her. That relationship must exist before you can effectively challenge someone. In other words, challenge doesn't exist in a vacuum. The relationship can be built quickly before the challenge is presented, but there must be a relationship in place. Think about when you interview a new applicant for a sales position. While you've just met the person, you challenge potential salespeople during the recruiting process because you're asking them tough questions. You challenge current team members to think bigger and set more ambitious goals for themselves. And you challenge people during the coaching review to be more open and honest about their fears, doubts and anxieties. The longer the duration of the relationship, the more you can ask for—and expect—from the people you're working with.

Establishing this relationship lets you move on to challenging someone. All of us have been challenged by others throughout our lives. As children, we're challenged by parents, teachers, siblings, friends, and coaches. As adults, we're challenged in both our personal and professional lives by spouses, co-workers, and bosses—sometimes even by our own kids. But as humans, we don't want to change. We want to stay in our snug little comfort zone. That's why when we're challenged, we often respond defensively. We say things like, "What does this person know?" "What right does he have telling me what to do?" "Why doesn't she mind her own business?" "Where did these comments come from?" "This is the last thing I need right now."

That kind of negative response is a natural reaction to challenge. However, when the challenge comes from someone we respect, we're more likely to listen. If not, the challenge itself will have little impact—possibly no impact—even if what the person is saying is correct.

Respect, and how to get it, is a hot topic in the world of business books. Successful sales coaches must inspire respect from those that they lead by demonstrating six key qualities. The more of these qualities that you have, the more respect you'll command from those you work with. These qualities are: vision, a history of success, continuous learning, empathy, vulnerability, and follow-through.

Vision

The most important factor in gaining another's respect is having an exciting vision that attracts people who also want to accomplish something worthwhile. This vision is more than just a goal. I've met many coaches who set goals and believe that the goals create a vision. But a goal alone is not a vision. A vision has an exciting goal as part of it, but it also includes the reasons for achieving the goal. Your vision should address the key behaviors that indicate what clients can expect from the organization, and a description of what about the organization makes it special.

On the following page, you'll find an exercise to help determine your personal vision for your department; answers have been filled in for a theoretical sales coach. Note that there are four elements to the vision: impact, core values, exceptional goal, and vivid description.

- *Impact* refers to what you do for others. It's how we make a difference in someone else's life. Recall that in Chapter One, you learned that making an impact is one of the motivating factors for many salespeople. As the sales coach, you must have a specific impact in mind.
- *Core values* are the attributes that are essential to how you conduct business. Clarifying your personal core values is important for several reasons. First, it helps you drill down to your personal work priorities, and gives you a standard to live up to. Identifying these core values also tells you what values to look for when interviewing candidates who will work for you. (You'll find more about how to uncover candidates' values in Chapter Three.)
- *Exceptional goal* is the specific objective you hope to accomplish. This goal should be SMART—specific, measurable, achievable, realistic, and time-oriented. Simply setting a goal of overall improvement isn't enough. You must have a specific goal that can be measured and has a timeframe. This exceptional goal should be ambitious but within your ability (and your team's) to accomplish.
- *Vivid description* is what you will see in place when the goal has been achieved. The vivid description can serve as a reference point to help you determine which strategies to use to accomplish the goal.

When you're thinking about your vision, keep in mind that anyone can get in front of a group that's already headed somewhere. An effective leader, however, creates a vision that attracts people to him or her.

Finally, there must be alignment between your professional vision and that of the company you work for. When your goals and values align, it will be a good "fit" for you and the company. If not, you'll be out of sync with the company and will have a more difficult time succeeding in that environment. The same is true for each of your team members. While their roles and their

Vision

IMPACT — *Why I am in business*

- To help people achieve their most important business goals

CORE VALUES — *How I will conduct business*

- Follow-through
- Challenge people to think
- Hard work and continuous learning
- Listening to understand

EXCEPTIONAL GOAL — *What I want to accomplish*

- Within three years, our team wins the company's award for exceptional growth

VIVID DESCRIPTION — *What I will see happening*

- Continuous skill and knowledge development
- Administrative staff in place to free up salespeople for more client contact
- Relationships with key vendors
- A network of contacts that benefits our firm and clients
- Membership in community organizations
- Team selling to penetrate difficult accounts
- Selling in new markets

contributions to the overall vision may differ, their personal visions and goals must mesh with the team's vision for each of them to succeed.

History of Success

A history of success can be a result of your own accomplishments as a salesperson, the results of other sales teams you've led, or of having been a part of an exceptional sales organization. As a new sales coach, you can quickly gain the respect of the people you lead by demonstrating your previous track record. Salespeople trust and respect one who has climbed the success ladder. The team knows that the coach's advice is based on his experience, not just from having read a book on sales coaching. (Though this book will certainly help you build that history of success!)

Sharing your previous successes is not bragging. It doesn't mean that you walk around broadcasting your accomplishments to anyone who will listen. But you already know how a person's reputation precedes him or her in any corporate environment. Chances are your history of success will be public knowledge, whether you want it to be or not; just don't be afraid to share those success stories when appropriate.

Continuous Learning

You can expect others to be willing to implement new learning when it is obvious that you, too, continue to learn. You've got to stay active in your field and continue to study and hone your skills. Once again, "walking the talk" will motivate the people who work for you.

Remember that according to the GRF, new learning is what creates results. Even if you have tremendous drive, the lack of the requisite knowledge will prevent you from reaching your goals. Continuous learning shows your team that you're always striving to educate yourself and expand your knowledge base.

In sales, you never know it all. Just working every day, you learn. The people you work with are complex, and the more experiences you have, the more you understand what makes people tick. While you might face situations that are similar to past experiences, every single sale, every client, and every encounter is different.

In addition to people skills, you have to keep up on the products you're selling. As the products are improved and changed, you must stay up to speed on how those features create benefits for clients. Where does the product fit in now? What are its current and future applications? The ever-changing, complex world of sales ensures that you're in for a lifetime of learning, and embracing that will inspire and motivate your team.

Empathy

Listening is one of the most important ways to show that you understand what a person is feeling and thinking. This is empathy. You want to understand what is going on with the person you're talking to. You demonstrate this by taking time to learn the salesperson's point of view or how he responds to an issue. An excellent coach is willing to listen and care; this personal touch is a significant key to the person's success.

But how do you do this? Even in a coaching session, there's a good chance that you're not listening attentively every minute. You may be distracted or preoccupied, or planning what you're going to say next instead of really paying attention to the person you're speaking with. This problem is compounded when you're on the phone and attempting to multi-task by checking up on e-mail or flipping through papers on your desk—neither of which I recommend!

Becoming an effective listener takes time and effort. As a coach, you should use active listening techniques, which let you confirm that you're receiving the message the person talking with you intends to communicate. You also listen in an open, non-defensive fashion, demonstrating vulnerability. Active listening focuses your attention on the person you're working with. This shows respect for the other person, builds trust, and helps avoid misunderstandings. It also helps deepen the other person's respect for you.

Your goal as an active listener is to understand the perspective of the other person, instead of assuming that it's identical to your own. You listen as a receiver, rather than as a critic. In short, the objective is to achieve agreement from or change in the person you're speaking with, instead of directing him or her to do something. And as you know now, that's what a successful coaching relationship is all about.

However, active listening can be easy to describe but tough to carry out. To become a better active listener, try these techniques:

- *Acknowledgment.* Show the person that you're listening by maintaining eye contact, and by nodding or offering verbal encouragers (such as "I see" or "Go on") when appropriate.

- *Paraphrasing.* Part of active listening is summarizing what has been said to you to give the person an opportunity to agree or disagree with it.
- *Probing.* This includes asking additional questions to clarify what the person is telling you, rather than simply accepting what the person has said.
- *Providing feedback.* Active listening involves more than listening. Give feedback that shows that you understand what the person is saying, and share your own relevant experiences to show your openness and to build trust.
- *Reflection.* When you reflect, you comment on the emotions or experiences that you perceive—for example, "It sounds like you're angry and frustrated about this situation." Your reflective comments can relate to the factual or emotional content that's being shared, but shouldn't attempt to definitively label the problem or emotion.
- *Silence.* Sometimes people need time to collect their thoughts or decide how to phrase something. Don't immediately jump in after the person says something; give her the opportunity to finish her thoughts, or add to what she has already said. A moment of silence after someone has stopped talking—instead of rushing in with your own comments (or worse yet, interrupting the person) makes the conversation less forced and again invites open, full disclosure.
- *Summary.* Finally, at the end of the conversation, you should summarize the discussion so that you're both clear on what was said and agreed to. It's also appropriate to summarize at the beginning of the conversation to remind the person where the two of you left off at an earlier meeting.

Most of us are empathetic to some degree, whether we express it or not. But active listening doesn't come naturally to most people. Most of us are wrapped up in telling our own stories or in making our point to be effective listeners. The best sales coaches, however, realize that good listeners tend to be powerful influencers of others. They also know that expressing empathy lets you connect emotionally with people, and encourages open, frank communication.

Vulnerability

Sales coaches and other people in positions of authority often fear appearing vulnerable, and I think that's a mistake. Vulnerability isn't a sign of weakness, but a sign of strength. You're admitting your shortcomings. Only a strong person—or one who's becoming a strong person—is able to do that.

Don't worry that being open means that people will take advantage of you. Openness lets you be aware of your shortcomings without feeling that you have to hide them, or worse, worry that they will be discovered. That fear leads to a tendency to be defensive, and you can't effectively challenge someone when you're on the defensive.

The bottom line is that a salesperson will be more open with another person when that person—the coach—demonstrates openness and vulnerability. Yes, your history of success is important. But when you're willing to share the struggles, fears and anxieties you've experienced, you're saying that you're like everyone else. By being open, you can better understand and empathize with the anxiety of others.

This doesn't mean that you air your dirty laundry or frighten the person you're coaching with personal stories that are better suited for your therapist. But a degree of openness and empathy (that you can demonstrate by using the active listening techniques I just discussed) lets you create a stronger relationship with your team members.

Let's say you're working with a relatively new team member who's struggling with making calls. He has a hard time not taking each rejection personally, and you can tell his enthusiasm for his work is flagging. Why not tell him about a similar situation you encountered—and how you handled it? The point isn't to brag or downplay the difficulty of the particular situation. It's to show that you've been there, and are willing to talk about your own fears and anxieties—and that they can be overcome. That's a much more effective way to connect with someone than simply telling them how you accomplished something and omitting its emotional, even negative, aspects.

Follow-Through

It's not enough to say that you'll do something. You do it. A successful coach understands the importance of follow-through. When you follow up on a commitment to the person you're working with, the salesperson knows that her needs and her success are important to you.

Follow-through also demonstrates drive and discipline. Recall in the last chapter that a person who's driven meets her commitments, regardless of how she feels or the obstacles in her way. This essential component of drive is one that you should demonstrate, too. How can you emphasize its importance to others if you yourself can't be relied on? Follow-through, also known as dependability, creates trust in the people you work with, and is an essential component of respect.

Understanding Challenge

Once you have the respect of the person you're going to challenge, you must consider how to approach that challenge. Almost all parents, teachers, coaches, and bosses challenge. It's part of their job descriptions, and these leaders see challenge as their responsibility. You've been challenged both as a child and as an adult, so you'll be familiar with many of the aspects of both positive and negative challenge. I'll start by discussing negative challenge so you can learn what it is and why not to use it—then you'll learn how to use positive challenge techniques.

What Negative Challenge Looks Like

Negative challenge is often a combination of preaching and lecturing. It varies in form and type, but in general is judgmental and critical, inappropriate, overwhelming, or one-sided—or some combination of all of these things.

Many negative challenges are personally demeaning. Comments such as, "What an idiot you are!" or "How could you do something like that?" or "What is wrong with you?" are all good examples. Statements like these belittle the person you're working with and destroy confidence. These statements are often judgmental as well, as in, "That's really stupid."

A negative challenge may be unrelated to what is important to the person you're challenging. If the salesperson isn't motivated by recognition and you keep pushing him to become more noticed in his field, the challenge is a negative one. (Of course, this might be a positive challenge for someone who is driven by the desire to be recognized by his peers.)

A challenge that overwhelms someone is also a negative one. Think about it. A coach may think that he's motivating someone using high-energy, rapid-fire commands, but they usually have the opposite effect. Think about someone telling you, "Go. Come on. Let's do it. Get going. Here's what's wrong with you. Do this. Do that. Do this." Your response is likely to be one of resistance, not commitment.

You can also tell a negative challenge by the fact that it's one-sided. A sales coach making a one-sided challenge isn't worried about what the salesperson is thinking, or what new learning may have to occur, or how to help the person deal with mistakes. He simply tells the person what to do and then moves on.

If you think about it, most people recognize that this approach doesn't work. Yet negative challenge is used more often than positive challenge, for a variety reasons. First, the challenger may have never learned another approach. If you grew up only hearing this kind of challenge from your parents, teachers, and others in authority, it's unreasonable to expect you to inherently know how to challenge in a positive fashion. It may not feel natural. But you can learn how to do it.

Keep in mind, too, that children usually don't have the option of escaping someone who negatively challenges them. They're stuck with their parents and teachers—for at least a year, in the latter case. But most adults won't put up with negative challenge for long. Treat your team like this, and chances are they'll quit and go to work for someone else.

Negative challenge is by its nature very controlling, and can give you a false sense of security. You feel like you're in control, and for the time being, you are. But you're actually *losing* control over how the person will act and react to you in the future. Negative challenge increases the chance that the person will not respond the way you want, or that he or she will decide to escape it altogether—by getting another job.

But it's easy to see why people use negative challenge. It's a way of avoiding the anxiety of a two-way conversation. You're likely to use it if you don't want to admit that you might be the cause of the problem, or even contributing to the problem. If you don't have a solution to the perceived problem, you feel weak, and slip back into the perceived control of negative challenge. Negative challenge can make you feel superior, but this feeling is fleeting.

In other cases, you may be rushed or lack the patience to fully discuss the issue. Failing to plan for this conversation and to give enough time for it to occur may result in negative challenge.

It's true that sometimes negative challenge works, which is one of the reasons sales coaches, use it. But it doesn't work consistently, and even when it does work, it increases the risk of alienating the people you work with.

Choosing to Change

Keep in mind that negative challenge can happen automatically. People who use negative challenge tend to be impatient and appear angry, even if they're not. If you feel angry, frustrated, or impatient when you're working with someone, you're probably challenging them in a negative way. Take a closer look at your own emotions. Anger and impatience have fear as their root causes—the fear that you might have to work harder and longer, or that you might lose your job if you can't get people to change.

How then do you keep from responding automatically? How can you change your challenging method from a style that is controlling, exhausting, and unfulfilling?

There are several solutions. First, you must explore and accept your own limitations. Admitting and accepting your limitations makes you open and vulnerable, and this vulnerability makes it easier to be accepting of others. This doesn't mean you settle for mediocrity; rather, you admit your inadequacies and choose to do something about them. In short, you have to give up your need to be omnipotent. You cannot be perfect, after all!

Second, you need to realize that failure is always a possibility. That's not the end of the world. If you do fail, you know what to do to recover from it—or you learn how to recover from it. To recognize that failure is a possibility might seem like a strange concept, especially if you have avoided it or never have had to recover from a major failure, but there are more than enough examples of people who have put their careers back together after business catastrophes. (In Chapter Six, you'll learn how to minimize the impact of fear and failure.)

Finally, you must remember that people are individuals and will not respond the same way to the same challenges. That's why knowing someone's GRF is critical. That number helps you determine how much to ask of the person you're working with, and not overwhelm him with unreasonable, even impossible, expectations.

Several years ago, I made this mistake with a salesperson. I left no stone unturned as I detailed all of the issues I perceived this person was struggling with. In my enthusiasm to help, I disregarded his relatively low GRF, and completely overwhelmed him. I found out later that he went back to his office and lay motionless on the floor for an hour, overcome by what I had said. Then he sought therapy to address some of these issues. This is not the way to challenge someone—and I learned my lesson. Giving too much information can overload someone, regardless of your intention. (See the graphic on the next page for the relationship between challenge and performance.)

That's why it's critical to challenge people one person at a time. You can't challenge the entire team all at once. Positive challenge is not a football coach giving the inspirational speech at halftime to encourage his team to make the comeback and win the game. Positive challenge takes time. It's not a pep talk. When you're focused on helping people change, you expect it to take time.

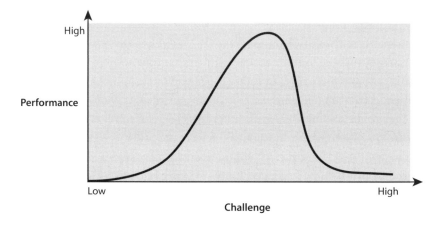

Figure 2.1: Performance/Challenge Relationship Model

Practicing Positive Challenge

So, now you know what negative challenge looks like. People who use it think they can sit down one time, read someone the riot act, and manipulate them through shame and guilt. Positive challenge, on the other hand, takes time and patience. You must understand the complexity of implementing major change to appreciate it, but when you begin to use it, you'll find that it's more effective and long-lasting than negative challenge.

Negative challenge tends to involve a lot of talking (and criticizing) by the person seeking change. With positive challenge, you start out introducing what you plan to do. For example, "We're going to talk about what's important to your success and really examine why you're behind on your goals." Note that the focus is on the two of you working together, without negative judgments or criticisms. It's also direct and specific, and immediately gets the salesperson involved in the process.

Positive challenge has nothing to do with judgment. With positive challenge, you stick with the facts and go from there. The next step is to ask the person to use self-diagnosis—in other words, how does she think she's doing? After you address defensive statements and behavior that may arise, you move toward defining the solution.

With positive challenge, you establish mutual goals—goals that both people agree on. In addition, both people agree to work toward the goals. This is where your follow-through as the coach can be critical to the salesperson's success. (Contrast this with the one-sided nature of negative challenge, where the person is directed to accomplish something, usually without the involvement or participation of the challenging party.)

Positive challenge involves focused discussion rather than accountability. Sales managers often talk about holding people "accountable" to their goals. Here's the problem with that concept. If the salesperson is behind on his goals, what can you do to hold him accountable? You can fine him, yell at him, or threaten some other type of negative consequence. Yet none of these actions address the reasons the person isn't meeting his goals.

Instead, the focused discussion helps you assist the salesperson in diagnosing the root cause of being behind on the goal. And, as you learned last chapter, the three main reasons are lack of drive, lack of new learning, and self-defeating thinking. But these problems can't be diagnosed without the salesperson's input. That's why you've got to get the person talking.

If he is making progress, you discuss what he is doing to obtain good results. If he is behind on the goal, he might become defensive. It's normal for people to complain, criticize, make excuses, and blame others. (Some people make a career out of it!) Most salespeople want to perform well and if they're failing to meet their goals, they may not be sure of the reasons.

The easy answer is to look outside of themselves for reasons, or rather, excuses. You've probably done this yourself. Often, there are external factors that get in the way of performance, but it's important to help the person focus on the internal reasons. To do this, you have to address the defensive behavior that may occur. First, show empathy by listening to the person and telling him, "I understand your point of view."

After you demonstrate empathy, you work toward a solution to both external and internal problems by asking this question: *"What can be done to solve the problem?"* This question forces the salesperson to focus on solving the problem. Each time you ask the question, you might continue to get a defensive response, so we must again demonstrate empathy and then ask the question again, *"What can be done to solve the problem?"*

The external bottlenecks that get in the way of performance are many and require real creativity. The internal problems are addressed in the GRF: drive, new learning, and self-defeating thinking. As a sales coach, it is your job to have a two-way discussion to work on a solution to the problem that both parties will commit to.

If the person refuses to accept responsibility and avoids discussion on how to solve the problem, you need to ask this question: "What are the consequences if you can't solve this problem?" The only way consequences will have any impact is if the person hears himself saying them. Be aware the first response might be, "Well, you could fire me." If you get that response say, "I could, but what other consequences are there well before being terminated?"

This forces the person to reflect more on the possible consequences. You might get comments like the following: "I will be letting you and the team down." "I won't get a raise." "I will be taken off this project." "I will be demoted." Once the salesperson verbalizes the consequences, he will often accept *his* responsibility for his actions.

Addressing Defensive Behavior

When you encounter defenses, you can use three basic strategies to deal with it. You can ignore the defensive behavior, agree with part of it, or refute it with contradictory evidence. Your reaction will depend on the situation and the defense raised, but there are some specific defenses that arise that you should be aware of. These types of defenses take the conversation off-track and away from problem-solving, and it's crucial to address them. As you work through them, you learn what kind of self-defeating thinking your salesperson has, and you can help her overcome it. This can take time—and patience.

The most common defenses include:

1. *Anger*

When you ask the salesperson what he is going to do to solve the problem, she becomes angry and might make a personal attack on you. In Chapter Five, you'll learn a strategy to handle criticism if the attack is directed at you. For now, remember that the root of anger is fear and helplessness. The angry person has learned that anger causes others to give in to the anger and, as a result, the angry person doesn't have to change.

If the anger is not directed at you, the following kinds of questions can help the person vent her anger so that you can discuss a solution: "What is bothering you?" "Is anything else bothering you?" "What are your fears?"

"What are you afraid will happen?" "What other factors are affecting your production?"

2. Crying

The socialization process tells men that crying is bad, while crying for women is acceptable. Even in a business setting, some women might cry when they become angry, frustrated, or hurt. Unfortunately, many coaches avoid dealing with this expression of emotion and end the conversation immediately.

To keep the conversation going, ask these questions: "What is bothering you?" "How are you feeling?" "What are you angry about?" Once the real problem is out in the open, you can address a solution. If a man cries in a business setting, realize he is emotionally spent. He believes the world is caving in around him and he will suffer severe consequences. In this situation, ask him what he's thinking and what he is afraid will happen. Encouraging both male and female salespeople to express their frustrations, whether they're crying or not, opens the way to solid communication.

3. Depression

Here, I'm speaking of the normal loss of energy that accompanies disappointment, not clinical depression. Here you notice that the person seems to be deflated and discouraged. The question to ask is, "What was the dream and what do you now see as reality? How can we turn disappointment into opportunity?"

4. Helplessness

When you ask the person what he can do about a particular problem, he tells you, "There's nothing I can do about that." This is someone who doesn't want to accept the responsibility for change. If you hear this, ask, "But what *could* you do to solve the problem?" You might get vague answers in response like, "I don't know," and if so, you have to continue asking the question until you start getting an answer.

If the person really doesn't know a solution to the problem because of his lack of knowledge, offer him several possible solutions and ask, "Which idea works for you?" Keep in mind that passive helplessness has been learned over time. If a salesperson is passive long enough, someone will give him an answer. Later, he'll tell the person that her idea didn't work. Giving options guards against this situation, and lets the salesperson choose the solution to employ.

Don't lose your temper with this person, either. That makes the helpless person feel powerful because he upset his boss—and he learns that this defense gives him control over your behavior.

5. Intellectualization

Here, the salesperson has a strong belief that she is right and nothing needs to be changed. She is so certain of what she believes that she may ignore all contradictory evidence. This salesperson might say something like, "This is the way things should be. This is a problem that will go away. I believe my way is the best one."

If you hear something like this, challenge those set beliefs. Ask, "Where did that belief come from?" and keep pressing her for an answer. It may take time, but when the salesperson realizes she has no real evidence to support her point of view, she will start looking for a solution both you and she can believe in.

6. Vagueness

When it's time to ask the salesperson if he is going to commit to the solution, he might say, "I think so" or "Probably." At this point, you have to push for a yes or no answer by saying, "Are you going to do this?" If he continues to give a vague answer, ask, "What problems might you encounter if you make the commitment?"

After he addresses the problems, you push for a yes or no answer to the question once more. "Are you going to do this?" If he can't say yes, that's a sign you're not really communicating. Move past the vagueness by having him tell you the reasons he's not going to do it, and then explore each of them with him.

By addressing the defenses that arise, you'll help the salesperson move toward a solution and overcome their self-defeating thinking as well. Remember that positive challenge, while time-consuming, is relatively simple to employ. It's no more than bringing up a problem that needs to be addressed, dealing with the normal defenses that go with confrontation, and working to determine a solution.

A Long-Term Process

The process of positive challenge doesn't end there, however. You'll continue to meet with the person over time, employing the same process, and helping the person move toward his goals and brainstorm solutions for the inevitable problems that will arise. Understanding that positive challenge is a process, not a one-time thing, is critical.

Years ago, when I was working with my own coach, I was on the road 150 nights a year to meet with clients. While I enjoyed traveling, I wanted to spend more time with my daughter. I considered cutting back on travel and going to phone appointments instead, but I agonized over the decision. I was afraid I wouldn't be as effective and that I'd lose clients and hurt my business if I cut back on my face-to-face meetings. If I made this transition, I'd have to figure out where I was going to set up my office, maintain my client records, minimize my losses, and continue to expand my business. (The irony is that at this point, my business had reached a plateau—I had clients calling me from different parts of the country, but it wasn't cost-effective to work with them face-to-face.) It took an entire year of discussing this transition with my coach for me to be able to cut back on travel and rely on phone appointments, rather than face-to-face meetings. During that process, my coach used positive challenge to keep me focused on making this change. The following year, I had a 25 percent increase in revenue, and many of the problems I thought I would encounter never materialized. Yet I might never have made the change had I not been challenged to confront my self-defeating thinking and start thinking bigger.

Let's consider another example. Let's say you're working with a consulting engineer who is bidding on a construction project for a municipality. This engineer is an excellent salesperson, but she's never dealt with the political situations inherent in city government. She needs to learn to build relationships with people in city government and on the city council. This is new to her, and it feels foreign. Creating those key relationships won't happen overnight, and you'll need to help keep her focused on achieving that goal over time. Positively challenging her to do so isn't a one-time sit-down, where you tell her what to do. Instead, it's a long conversation over time about making the change.

Worried that you don't have the luxury of time to make these changes? Give yourself and the people you work with more time. Remember we're talking about helping good people get better here—people who have great potential but aren't living up to it. If you're working with someone who consistently underperforms, has little or no motivation to change, and who you believe isn't going to change, then positive challenge may not work. In that case, terminating the person's employment may be the most appropriate option.

To sum up, positive challenge doesn't mean yelling, accusing, or use using shame, guilt, or fear to bring about a change in behavior. While these methods might work sometimes, if you use them frequently you'll lose the respect of the people you coach. And now you know that respect is critical to bringing about change in your salespeople.

3

Identifying and Attracting Talent

Key concept: The best sales leaders attract the best salespeople.

In the last chapter, you learned about the elements of positive challenge, and why the people you work with must respect you. In some instances, you'll work with people who were hired or recruited by someone else. But as a sales coach, you're often responsible for interviewing and hiring new members of your team. In this chapter you'll learn how to identify salespeople with the potential and drive to be extremely successful, and reduce your risk of making a bad hiring decision.

In the world of sales, people move from one company to another for one of three reasons—leadership, platform, or money. Leadership is your attraction power and ability to be a personal resource to the salesperson. Platform refers both to the type of product you're selling and the company resources that help you be more effective at sales, and money is the short- and long-term income potential. You may not be able to do a lot about these two elements, but as a sales coach, you can (and should) demonstrate leadership to the people who work for you—and to the people who you want to work for you. Spending the time to conduct an in-depth interview helps establish you as a leader from the outset, and will help you recruit salespeople with significant potential to your team.

So, your candidate is likely to be someone who wants to work for better money, for a better company, or for a better leader. That third element is completely within your control.

Keep in mind that there aren't many top performers looking to change the company that they're working for. Your most promising candidate may not be a superstar with an impressive background. Rather, he or she is someone whom you like and want to work with to achieve a common goal.

Hiring managers use a variety of techniques to try to learn more about job candidates and their skills, and you probably have your own methods of identifying successful salespeople. Sometimes those methods work, and sometimes they don't. I wish there was a test that could determine with 100 percent accuracy that the person you were recruiting could not fail; unfortunately, I haven't found one.

What I have developed is a series of assessment tools that provide valuable insight into the candidate's personality and can assist you in developing more effective questions to determine if he or she is someone you want to coach. If you hire a particular candidate, the information you gather from the assessment tools will make you a better coach for that person.

Let me clarify that what I'm talking about in this chapter isn't the first initial interview where you just get to know the individual, learn a little bit about her background, or give her some selection tests. You may not even be involved at that stage.

This interview is an in-depth process designed to help you understand the candidate to determine whether you like each other and want to work together. Presumably, an initial interview has already occurred, and the purpose of this next step is to determine whether there's a good fit between the two of you. This in-depth interview should occur before you start discussing the candidate's future career and how your company can help her achieve her goals. Describing what resources are available within the company and what your compensation plan looks like are irrelevant at this stage. Before you take that step, you have to spend time with the candidate to consider whether you like her, and whether you can work with her. In other words, the chemistry has to be right.

I was reminded of the importance of chemistry when my daughter was selecting a college. She's a sprinter and hurdler who excelled at track in high school. As a senior, she knew she wanted to continue to compete, and had a lot of colleges to select from. After considering many colleges, she decided to attend the school where she felt like she "fit" with the track coach, Stephanie

Domin at Carthage College in Kenosha, Wisconsin. My daughter was concerned with the overall program and what the workouts would be like. But her priority was that there was good chemistry between her and the coach. She knew that if the chemistry was there, she would be able to work with the coach to attain her athletic goals.

Looking for Potential

My daughter was looking for a coach who could help her develop her athletic potential. As the sales coach, you're looking for coachable people who you can help develop their selling potential. These people may not be easy to identify—unless they're already at the top of their games.

In Chapter One, I mentioned that according to evolutionary psychologists, only ten percent of the population has a clear vision of what they want. The other ninety percent—the vast majority—want to work for somebody with a clear vision. In other words, one out of every ten people you interview will be a visionary, while the other nine are looking for a visionary they can join.

Note that the visionaries don't need a lot of help. The visionary is really an individual who has high drive, minimal self-defeating thinking, and needs to master area(s) of new learning. If you help visionaries continue to learn, this small percentage of your sales force is going to get results regardless of what you do. It's the other ninety percent that you can impact.

As you go through the selection process, it can be easy to recognize the superstars. They're the top producers who have incredible drive and energy, but these superstars make up the minority of your team. Your job is to identify hidden talent—in this case, the people who can develop and grow and achieve far more than they thought they could on their own, with the help of an effective sales coach.

Paul "Bear" Bryant, the legendary football coach at Alabama, was once asked about how he put winning teams together. According to Bryant, the key concept was "in-betweeners." His teams weren't successful because he had superstar players—only a handful of his players were record-setting athletes. It was the other players—the former high school athletes who would never play professional football, but who could be developed into strong, reliable athletes—that made the difference. When Bryant recruited high school players, he looked for young men who might lack superstar talent, but who had something just as important—the ability to make a huge contribution to his team.

That's what I'm talking about here. You're looking for the in-betweeners to help you create a winning team. As a sales coach, I do most of my work in the financial services industry. For new, inexperienced salespeople, some companies that sell life insurance and other investment products have an average retention rate of only ten percent after five years. In other words, ninety percent of the salespeople who are brought into a financial services company don't make it.

Employee retention rates vary from industry to industry, but retention of successful salespeople is an issue for nearly every company. That's an enormous waste of time, money, and corporate resources, and it's one of the reasons why hiring the right people is so critical. When you hire people you can successfully coach, you can improve your team's retention rate.

In fact, people who I have worked with and who have mastered the in-depth selection interview process to select their team members have extremely high retention and productivity rates among their sales team members. As a sales coach responsible for your team's success, that's what you want as well.

The Profile of the Ideal Candidate

Before we get into the interview process itself, let's take a look at the hypothetical ideal candidate. Obviously, you want to consider how the person presents himself and his work history. Yet this alone isn't a guarantee of future performance. Consider the world of professional sports, and the large number of athletes who get drafted onto major sports teams, but who wash out. For whatever reason, they just can't fit in with the team or handle the pressure of what they are expected to do.

The same thing is true here, even though a personal history of success is an important criterion to consider. But you need to look at more than just that and determine whether the person you're interviewing has the following characteristics:

Coachability

Is this candidate open to opportunity? In other words, is this potential candidate coachable? Is he willing and open to ideas from others, or is he independent and autonomous? In order to be successful, a candidate must overcome self-defeating thinking by being open, honest, and vulnerable to others. The behavioral trait questions in the Appendix are designed to elicit answers that indicate if the candidate can admit vulnerability, and you'll find other questions to help determine coachability later in this chapter. Remember, a person must be able and willing to be vulnerable to be coached—otherwise you won't be able to help him overcome the normal anxiety that goes with change. Being coachable is a must!

History of Achievement

If you as the sales coach want to achieve exceptional goals and be at the top of your peer group, the people on your sales team must want the same outcome. The best indicator of potential high achievement is if the candidate has previously been a top performer in a sales group, or if he has climbed to the top of his peer group through continuous learning. In other words, the person may be coming from a different career, but has always excelled at whatever he has chosen—he's been recognized as an outstanding teacher or a highly successful retail manager, for example.

A lack of sales experience or leadership experience doesn't mean your candidate can't be successful at sales. When I was in high school, we held magazine drives to raise money for class trips, and I was never particularly successful at them. I did the minimum required to qualify for the trip. I didn't like to sell, and never saw myself as a salesperson. As an adult, though, I overcame that limitation with coaching and the fact that I did want to have a better quality of life, which is one of the traits of an ideal candidate.

Desire for an Exceptional Quality of Life

An organization needs money to fund growth. If the potential candidate isn't interested in exceeding the starting salary to fund his lifestyle, you are in trouble. The Balanced Goal Exercise in the Appendix can help you determine if the candidate needs more money to create the quality of life he wants. Some candidates might never have thought about personal goals for themselves or their families before and, if this is the case, you can gain the respect of the candidate by helping him start to consider these goals. The Balanced Goals Exercise can help you determine whether a candidate has a strong desire to make more money to achieve the lifestyle he wants.

Experience with "No"

Does the candidate have a history of putting himself in situations where he encounters a lot of personal rejection and disappointment? Job security for a salesperson is his ability to get new clients. Sourcing names and calling these prospects is what top salespeople do to grow their books of business. It is this ability to initiate contact uninvited with new potential clients that separates the top salespeople from the average performers.

A lack of a history of handling no doesn't mean you, as the sales coach, cannot help him deal with rejection. However, if he doesn't have experience with frequent rejection and does not appear to be coachable, you are taking a real risk in hiring this person.

Personality

Throughout the selection interview, you are engaging in a conversation with the candidate. Having a conversation is what sales is all about, so you have to ask yourself, "Am I enjoying talking to this person?" You're looking for someone who's personable, easy to talk to, and who you feel comfortable with. If you're not enjoying this brief conversation, you know this person isn't right for your team.

In the last chapter, you learned that people change when they get constant challenge from someone they respect. As a sales coach, I know that if I'm going to spend a lot of time helping someone achieve their goals, I want to be sure that this is an individual that I enjoy communicating with. You should keep the same approach in mind.

The In-Depth Selection Interview

Either you or another member of your management team has done some preliminary screening of the candidate to see if he has the minimum skills, knowledge, and experience to be an asset to your sales team. You've probably also had the candidate complete assessment instruments that give you additional insight into his ability to be successful in your business. Now that you know that the candidate has passed the initial screening process, it is time for an in-depth interview to see if this person will be a fit on your team.

The agenda for an in-depth interview includes the following steps:

1. Rapport-building;
2. Purpose and process;
3. Sales coach's background and vision;
4. Candidate's background;
5. Values and goal identification;
6. Employment history review;

7. Behavioral traits identification;
8. Coachability assessment;
9. Assessment of ability to handle "no";
10. Candidate's questions; and
11. Determining the next step.

Step One: Rapport-Building

The first step is building rapport between you and the person you're interviewing. This starts to build the relationship before you get into what is a stressful process—the actual job interview. The whole idea of rapport-building is to make the other person feel comfortable with you.

Look for things you have in common with the person throughout the interview process. Do you share the same friends? Do you have similar backgrounds? Do you have some similar interests? The process of rapport-building is just a way of saying, "I'm like you—you're like me," and it makes for a more open, relaxed environment.

Years ago, I met with a potential client in his office. The client had paintings on the wall of Navy fighter planes and I asked where they'd come from. When he said that he'd painted them, I told him I had a friend who was mentioned in a book I'd recently read called *"Kill" Migs* about aces in Vietnam. I was surprised when the man I was talking to said, "I wrote that book!"

From that moment on, the chemistry between the two of us was tremendous. There was no relationship tension, and we were able to talk about a variety of personal things because we spent time building rapport. It's not always easy to create this kind of rapport, but looking for things you have in common helps set the stage for open communication.

What are you doing to make the person feel comfortable? What do you share in common? What are the things you can talk about for five minutes in the beginning that help break the ice? Once you sense the candidate is feeling relaxed, then you can state your purpose and process for the interview.

Step Two: Purpose and Process

State the purpose and process by saying, "We are here so you can determine if this organization can help you achieve the quality of life you want. I hope to find out if you have the qualities necessary to help this organization achieve our vision. During this process, I will share with you my vision, what I want to accomplish as the coach of this team, and answer any question you have about my vision, this organization, and me. Then I'd like to find out more about you and your background. By the end of this meeting, we will both know what a next step might be." Using such a direct approach clarifies for the candidate your purpose, process, and intended outcome.

The basic purpose of this in-depth interview is to see if the two of you can help each other achieve your goals. You might even be so direct as to say that, "This is to see if we really like each other. There is no sense of us spending a lot of time if we don't think we like each other." This may be a pretty direct thing to say, but it is true.

Step Three: Sales Coach's Background and Vision

The next step is to share your background and vision so the candidate gets a general sense of who you are and what makes you tick. This gives him a reference point. Tell the person about your background, your career successes and failures, and your vision for the future. Then ask if he has any questions about you and your background. His questions (or lack of them) provide insight into his preparedness and his goals.

Step Four: Candidate's Background

Opening with, "Tell me about you," allows the candidate to share his previous successes and failures. Hopefully, he is going to tell about his strengths and weaknesses. Many candidates are only going to reveal their positive attributes; if you get a candidate who gives a balanced view of himself (including both strengths and weaknesses), then you know this candidate has a sense of security and is coachable.

When you ask an open-ended question like, "Tell me a little more about yourself," you could hear many things about the individual. What you're looking for, to some degree, is what the person doesn't say. Does he not mention anything about his family? Does he fail to mention any interests outside of work? Does the person seem afraid to even bring them up?

Now, some coaches avoid these kinds of questions because they're afraid they're getting into a dangerous area. Obviously, you don't want to ask illegal questions that concern someone's age, marital status or religion. A general, open-ended question like "Tell me about you" can lead into those areas; if it does, bring the interview back to the person's professional life and focus on his or her career. Or narrow your question slightly by asking something like, "How did you get where you are today?" or "Tell me more about your professional career."

This is an important area to cover even with a salesperson that has had a tremendous history of success. I remember I once interviewed a top salesperson from a financial services company who spent thirty minutes telling me all about accomplishments that I already knew about. At the end of those thirty minutes, I asked, "What were your reasons for telling me about things that I already knew?" It caught him off-guard, and it also told me that despite his achievements, he was an insecure individual. Even though at first glance, he appeared invulnerable (and was in fact extremely driven), my question revealed that he was insecure and vulnerable—and therefore, coachable. So remember, it's not only what the person tells you, but what he doesn't tell you that can be revealing and also indicate coachability.

Step Five: Values and Goal Identification

As the sales coach, you want to determine if the candidate shares many of the same values that you and your team do. To help identify values, ask the person to share three or four key decisions he has made in his life. Most decisions are value-based, so as you listen to his answers, you will begin to identify his values. Or you can ask him to identify the values that influenced each of the decisions.

You can work through the exercise with the candidate during the in-depth interview, or provide the values exercise at the initial interview and ask him to complete it and return it at the in-depth interview. I have clients who successfully use both approaches. You'll find the Values Exercise, along with a list of values, in the Appendix, page 128.

The Values Exercise is important because it lets you explore the candidate's values and see if they mesh with the organization's. Once, I was doing some team-building in an organization, and we did a Values Exercise for the eight sales leaders who were participating. The most important value for seven of the eight people in the room was career/financial rewards; the eighth person said that family was his number one value. When the sales leaders began talking about strategies and what they wanted to do about the future, the individual whose family was the number one value always would resist the ideas that were brought up during that process. He never said that implementing the strategies would interfere with or take time away from his family. But he fought them because he knew that using them would require more time and working in the evenings when they were first implemented. This is why knowing your candidate's values from the outset is so important.

When I went into business for myself in 1983, my key values were independence, autonomy, simplicity, and mastery. These were the values that caused me to get into the career that I'm in. However, there was something missing, and that was the need for money to pay the bills! On the day I entered business for myself, I had independence and autonomy. I also had simplicity and mastery because I didn't have anybody telling me what to do, and I spent time doing things that I thought would make me a better coach. In my previous job as a school administrator and athletic coach, I had never worked for money. I wanted to do good work, and as a result, I got paid. I didn't realize that being in business for myself meant that I had to put a plan in place to make money. I made the naïve assumption that just doing good work would create enough money to live on. Once I realized that I had to decide how much money I needed to get the quality of life I wanted, my business started to grow. The amount of money needed helped me face the reality that I needed a system to get new clients.

To avoid making the mistake of not knowing how much money a candidate needs to pay for the quality of life he wants, I suggest you use the Balanced Goals Exercise, which you'll find in the Appendix, page 130. You can do this exercise during the in-depth interview or hand it out at the initial interview and ask the candidate to complete it and bring it back for the in-depth interview. This exercise gives you and the candidate a good idea of what is important in all six areas of his life. In addition, he must list his three most important goals and explain what he will need to earn to pay for the lifestyle he wants.

As you do this exercise with a candidate, you want to consider what goals the person has and what things he wants for himself and his family that will require him to make significantly more money than he is currently making. After your candidate identifies the goals he wants to achieve in the six areas of life listed, ask him to pick out the three most important goals, write down why they are important, and then predict what their income needs to be in three to five years to achieve that quality of life. The candidate's values may be consistent with yours. He may be interested in growth, new learning, being on time, mastering his career, adding value, and being of service to individuals. These are all wonderful values, but if the person doesn't also have the desire for an exceptional quality of life—which the Balanced Goal Exercise identifies—this is a significant issue for a potential candidate. A client of mine who uses this exercise with all the candidates that he interviews finds that just using this exercise alone identifies people who have the potential to grow. He gives candidates a copy of the Balanced Goal Exercise and asks each person to complete it before the two of them meet for the in-depth interview. Some individuals return for the following interview, and say, "What Balanced Goal Exercise? You never gave me one." That tells you quite a bit about how organized this individual is.

At the other extreme, this client had a candidate who didn't just complete the two-page exercise; he provided the sales coach with a ten-page document of what he wanted to accomplish in his life. The sales coach wound up recruiting this individual, and he was one of the best first-year salespeople that his organization ever had. Identifying who this person is not only from a values perspective but also a goals perspective gives you an indication of whether this person fits into your organization and has the drive for an exceptional quality of life.

Step Six: Employment History Review

When reviewing the candidate's employment history, you want to discuss two key areas. One is the reason he left each job. Was he changing jobs to advance or to get away from something? Second, ask him to describe each of his bosses. As you hear the answer, listen to whether he gives the positive *and* negative characteristics or traits of each person. If he only gives the negative, there is a great likelihood you will be the next person he describes negatively! If the comments are only positive about each person, you might question the candidate's ability to be truthful because few bosses are perfect.

Step Seven: Behavioral Traits Identification

There are ten behavioral trait questions to explore with each candidate:

1. Motivation/work ethic;
2. Relationship-building ability;
3. Ability to influence people;
4. Assertiveness;
5. Awareness;
6. Problem-solving;
7. Energy creation;
8. Goal-setting;
9. Coping; and
10. Decision-making.

You'll find questions to ask about each of these behavioral traits in the Appendix, page 132.

For each trait, you'll find two questions that ask the candidate how he has positively demonstrated the specific trait. Then there is one question that asks when he hasn't been successful in exhibiting the trait. The purpose of asking the negative question is to determine if the candidate can be vulnerable, which you'll recall is a sign of being coachable as well.

For example, the questions for motivation/work ethic are:

1. Tell me when you were able to provide your own motivation, even though you were working alone.
2. Tell me about a goal you achieved that required long hours.
3. Tell me about a time in your life when you lacked motivation.

A prospective employee who is secure with himself can admit his mistakes. Asking both the positive and negative question gives you insight into his strengths and weaknesses. After you ask the three questions for each trait, give the candidate a rating of 1 to 10, with 10 being best. By rating each of the ten traits and adding the scores together, you now have an overall rating from 10 to 100. This rating can help you evaluate and compare all the candidates on a more objective basis. Also, by looking at scores over a period of time and seeing how the salesperson actually performs once he is hired, you can establish a benchmark that can make your selection process more accurate.

The other thing to be aware of as you listen to the candidate's answers is whether he meets your behavioral expectations. All of us have basic expectations of others that vary from person to person. If your pet peeve is people who are late and your candidate admits he often is tardy coming to meetings, you may have a hard time liking him. Being aware of your own expectations and finding out if the candidate reflects them can prevent hiring a good performer who might not be coachable.

The behavioral trait questions take a lot of time. That's why if you've gotten through the employment history and don't think the candidate is a good fit for you and the organization, you may decide to end the interview then, and let the candidate know you'll be in touch. If, however, this is an individual that you really want to spend more time with, then you can get into the behavioral trait questions in the Appendix.

Step Eight: Coachability Assessment

As I mentioned earlier, coachability is an essential attribute for a successful candidate to have. Two questions that can help you determine whether the candidate is coachable are: "What is your best guess of how former teachers, coaches, or club leaders would describe you?" and "What's your best guess about how former employers would describe you?" The candidate who shares both positive and negative traits reveals vulnerability and coachability; if he doesn't list any negative characteristics, you may not be able to coach him. Note, too, that if his descriptions of high school and college teachers and coaches are different from the descriptions of people from his career, you need to explore the reasons for the differences.

While these two questions are pretty self-explanatory, let me share my own answers if I were asked these questions today. My high school teachers and coaches would describe me as quiet, unassuming, and under-achieving; someone who did what he had to (but not much more), didn't make waves, and didn't demonstrate much in the way of leadership, but contributed to the team. But if you asked some of my first employers how they would describe me, they'd say goal-driven, motivated, and does what he needs to do to get the job done. If you hear a difference between school and work, ask about it. The difference for me was finding a goal, something that I wanted to do that I could commit to.

I wasn't alone, either. There are plenty of "lost souls" in college. Until you find a goal that creates drive to learn new things and overcome obstacles, it's easy to just go through the motions. So again, a high school or college record doesn't always indicate what a person might do once they get into the work force.

Another valuable question to explore this area is: "Who are the people who have had the most impact on your life and what type of relationship did you have with them?" What you're looking for in the answer is whether the relationship included a two-way conversation or just the significant person telling the candidate what to do. Explore whether the candidate could be totally open and honest in sharing his fears, doubts, anxieties, and mistakes with that individual. If he was, he's already had a coaching relationship, whether or not it was called that.

The coachability issue is probably the single most important factor addressed in the in-depth interview. Think of individuals who have tremendous talent but can't get along with the coach, and the impact that this has on an organization and the conflict that it creates. A person who isn't coachable is an incredible stressor on both the coach and on the coach's ability to maintain relationships with other salespeople. In addition, a coach with an uncoachable team member is going to have to resist the temptation to compromise key procedures, guidelines, rules, or regulations to please the one team member at the expense of the rest of the team's morale. That's why coachability is so important to you as the sales coach responsible for your team's success.

Step Nine: Assessment of Ability to Handle "No"

Simply ask the candidate whether he has put himself in situations where he had to encounter a lot of personal rejection. If he has had limited experience in this area, it doesn't mean he shouldn't be hired. As long as you feel he is coachable and you know he has a high amount of drive to succeed, you know this candidate will be a good match for your team.

Step Ten: Candidate's Questions

It's likely that the candidate will have questions for you, but only answer the ones that are related to you, your vision, or were generated throughout the interview process from the candidate. He may ask questions about you and how you handle different situations. What if he has conflict with you as a coach? Will you be able to work through that? What guidelines do you have for him? Even things as simple as coming to meetings or showing up for educational events can be discussed.

Remember the in-depth interview is to determine if you and the candidate can work together to achieve mutual goals. Any questions about the routines of the job, salary expectations, and the like can be addressed in the next meeting, if there is one.

Step Eleven: Determining the Next Step

If you like the candidate, suggest taking the next step in the interview process. If you aren't sure if there is a fit, tell the candidate you will get in touch with him by a specific date. When you do call him back, be honest and say there doesn't seem to be a fit.

Now you've got a framework for conducting the in-depth interview. Its purpose is five-fold. You want to use the process to:

1. Start to earn the respect of the candidate by the quality of your interview;

2. Determine if the candidate has similar core values to you and your organization;
3. Determine if the candidate has exceptional goals;
4. Discover if the candidate has enough of the key behavioral traits to be successful in your organization; and
5. Determine if the candidate is coachable.

You already know that there aren't many superstars walking around looking for new jobs. You might get lucky and have one show up for an interview, but that is rare. Your job is to use the in-depth interview process to find out if potential candidates share similar values and goals, but most importantly, you want to find out if they are coachable. If they are, you can challenge them to accomplish more than they thought was possible. One of my clients, an extremely successful sales coach, says that his role is to help people see ability in themselves that they've never seen before, to perform at a level they never thought was possible, and to achieve things they never thought they could.

That's a wonderful description of an effective sales coach's job. Anyone can coach salespeople who are already exceptional performers. The talented sales coach identifies and attracts salespeople who are personable, coachable and want a much better quality of life.

4

The Power of Focus

Key concept: The coach's job is to create and focus energy.

Nothing happens without energy. Car engines don't run without fuel. Lamps don't turn on without electricity. And people don't pursue a goal unless they have the drive to do so. It's your job as a coach to create and focus energy in the salespeople who work for you.

Remember the moon mission I mentioned earlier? In this case, the scientists at NASA were tremendously driven, but they had to learn a lot. They had to create enough energy in the form of rocket power to overcome gravity. They had to learn about guidance systems equipment, what to expect in outer space, and how to train people to cope with it.

Overcoming gravity is what got us to the moon, and it's no different for salespeople. They need the drive—the energy—to move to the next level, and they need new learning to cover the gap between where they're currently at, and where they want to be in terms of meeting customer needs, selling, and learning product knowledge. As they make these changes, they also need to overcome self-defeating thinking that causes them to wonder, "Is this change worth it? Do I really want to do this? Can I deal with the anxiety of the change?"

It's up to you to help create energy that will cause people to learn more, and at the same time overcome the self-defeating thinking that is holding them back. You'll employ similar strategies with all salespeople, but the way you approach them will depend on where they are in their careers.

Phase One: Survival

In phase one; salespeople are brand new to the career. They've never sold before, they've never worked for this company, and they've never solved many of the problems they'll face. These new salespeople may draw a salary in addition to commission, or work for 100 percent commission. Regardless, when they're new, they realize they have to be good enough to earn the amount of money they're making, or they'll find themselves out of a job.

This is survival mode. Salespeople worry whether they'll get good enough, fast enough, to avoid termination. The coaching that you use in this phase is the same as with the other two. However, salespeople in survival phase are more likely to divert from (or ignore entirely) what you tell them. They're likely to do what *they* think is necessary to survive, even though we have better insight into what they should do.

Consider it this way—as a sales coach, you're operating from logic. These salespeople may be operating from fear, and that fear may mean that they do the wrong thing. They also may be completely unaware of what they need to do next, so your role here includes teaching and identifying specific tactics for them to employ to reach their goals and help them overcome their self-defeating thinking. In addition, you'll need to touch base with them frequently to make sure they're on track—and if not, head them in the right direction again.

Phase Two: Stability

Once salespeople make it through the survival period, they move into a period of stability. Here, the salesperson feels that he's making enough money to justify his salary, or if he's paid by commission, enough to cover his minimum bills at home. At this point, salespeople feel safe. They're stable. They're not afraid of losing their jobs anymore. Yet even if they enjoy being at this stage, it's not enough.

There may be drive (even if it's unrecognized drive) to move to the next level, but the drive is a little bit different now. The drive isn't strictly about money. In fact, many salespeople struggle with the idea of making money. But to achieve new goals, salespeople will have to conquer aspects of new learning. In the stability mode, they may resist it. After all, if they feel comfortable, why should they want to learn this new information—let alone learn it quickly? Here, your job is to help people take more risks, and find some unmet need that will create energy—and therefore, drive.

Phase Three: Success

The next phase we get into is success. At this point, salespeople know a lot, and because of that learning, they're making more money than they need to pay their basic bills. At this particular phase, salespeople usually have more money than they need for day-to-day living. They're setting aside money for retirement, funding their children's education, and the like. Here, it's not meeting just the basic needs; at this stage, most salespeople have more income than they thought possible.

The real issue for the sales coach at this time is to help people figure out what's going to drive them to get to the next level. There's less emphasis on new learning at this point, and these people don't have a lot of self-defeating thinking. They've dealt with a lot. They're tougher mentally, because they've dealt with adversity. The question for them is, "Why do I want to continue to learn and grow? Why do I want to change? I'm pretty happy right where I am."

Regardless of what stage the salesperson you're working with is in, you're still dealing with energy creation. That requires increasing drive, limiting self-defeating thinking, or both. As the sales coach, you help bring about the energy to get through survival; the energy to move to stability; the energy to move to a state of success; and finally, the energy to continue to thrive in the success stage. People need help progressing through these stages, and the tools in this chapter are designed to do that.

Focus Tools

And what are these tools? The Focus Document, the Breakthrough Learning Document, and the Coaching Review. Briefly:

- The Focus Document is a one-page business plan that creates drive and identifies the key strategies (new learning) to achieve an exceptional goal;
- The Breakthrough Learning Document is a time-oriented tactical plan that includes the action steps necessary to implement the strategy and overcome self-defeating thinking.
- The Coaching Review is the agenda for follow-up meetings to make sure the breakthrough is accomplished. This is discussed in the next chapter.

The Focus Document

The Focus Document helps create energy. It helps identify necessary new learning and the support that will accelerate it. A completed Focus Document is on page 75 and a blank copy is in the Appendix, page 142. Its elements include:

- Purpose—"What I do for my clients."
- Value—"What separates me from other salespeople."
- Payoff—"What I get as a result of achieving my purpose."
- Needs—"What I don't have enough of."
- Key goals—"What I must do to get what I need."
- Key strategies—"How I will go about achieving the goal."
- Support—"What I need from others to help me perform at my best."

The first five sections of the Focus Document all address drive. Recall that people have different reasons for wanting to make change. The salesperson may have a need for money, recognition, impact, mastery, or belonging—or a combination of these things. Pursuing these needs create drive—and you know that continued growth is the result of drive and new learning minus the interference of self-defeating thinking.

Purpose

The question of purpose addresses impact; in other words, "What am I doing for other people? How am I impacting individuals?" Keep in mind that when you are working with a brand new salesperson who is in survival mode, she's not even thinking about what she's doing for other people. She's much more focused on whether she's going to hit her goals and make enough money to keep her job. Yet this can often be an internal struggle for many salespeople because they don't want their clients or prospects to think they are only in it for the money.

As an experienced sales coach, you know that if you help enough people get what they want, *you* will get what you want. A person in survival mode is not thinking about that. She is thinking about herself, so when you use the Focus Document with a new salesperson, you may have to explore what her purpose is. What problems is she solving for her clients? Why is it important to solve those problems? If you can do that well, you'll make money. But the primary reason we're in sales isn't to make money—our true purpose is to help people solve their problems. (And as a result of excelling at that, you make money.) Even salespeople in the stability and success stages sometimes forget what their real purpose is. You may have to remind them of that, and bring them back to the concept of how they are impacting people.

Value

The idea of "value" is really a mastery issue. It's what separates the salesperson from others in her field. Identifying what this is will help the salesperson live her purpose more effectively and make her able to help more people solve their problems. In the survival stage, the salesperson may not even know what she is good at. She hasn't had enough experience. In stability, the salesperson is getting better and may be trying to identify what he does well. And in the success stage, the salesperson usually knows what sets him apart from his peers.

Payoff

Payoff is what the salesperson gets as a result of achieving her purpose. Again, this gets back to what creates drive. Is she getting money for achieving this? Is she getting recognition? Is she getting a sense of making a difference? Does she have a feeling of mastery about what she does?

If the salesperson is in survival mode, the payoff is probably just to pay her bills. If the salesperson is in the stability mode, the payoff may be to continue to maintain where she's at. And at the success stage, the payoff may be more intangible. Regardless, I've found that many clients, regardless of what stage they're at, aren't really clear on what their purpose is and what separates them from other people. They're not sure of the benefits that they are providing.

If that's the case, you can suggest that they ask some of their best clients a series of questions. This is a great exercise to use with people who are established in sales but who don't seem to have the same drive as they used to. If it seems that they are just going through the motions, getting these questions answered can really energize people to become more successful, and it can also help to create drive.

Suggest that the salesperson call a handful of their top clients, and say something like, "I'm working with a marketing consultant who has asked me to ask four questions of several of my clients. I'd really appreciate your time, and the answers to these questions will help me help more people. Is there a convenient time to get together to go over them?"

The four questions are:

1. How do you explain to somebody else what I do?
2. What problems have I helped you solve?
3. What have been the benefits to you of our working together to solve these problems?
4. What skills or abilities do I have that you value the most?

The answers to these questions will help the salesperson identify her purpose and it will also give the salesperson a genuine feeling of fulfillment and accomplishment. Continuing to do this with more clients can create a lot more drive. An interesting part of this exercise is that salespeople will often get different answers from different clients. The answers can also help salespeople clarify how they can help their current customers solve more problems.

Needs

The next element on the Focus Document is needs. The salesperson should ask, "What don't I have enough of? What's missing in my life that I want to have more of?" If this question makes the salesperson feel greedy or self-centered, remind him that he has to help other people solve their problems if he is to meet his own needs. There's a fine balance between meeting other people's needs and meeting your own.

I often mention this to new salespeople by saying, "If a customer says to you, 'I think you're only in it for the money,' how would you respond?" A new salesperson will say, "How does he know I'm in it for the money? I need this sale to make this month's mortgage." This becomes very stressful for the salesperson, who doesn't know how to respond.

So, here's an appropriate answer to that question: "You're right—I am in this for the money. But you are only half-right because I can't make a dime until I help you solve a problem that you say is important to you. So why don't we get back to that problem?" This can help the salesperson feel more comfortable and confident, and remind him that he won't meet his own needs for money, recognition, mastery or a sense of belonging until he helps other people get what they want first.

I would tell him to remember that even though his needs are being met to some degree by living out his established purpose, that isn't enough for the long term. The needs for money, recognition, mastery, impact, and a sense of belonging to an exceptional team are constantly changing.

Key Goals

My experience working with salespeople reveals that there are really only two goals to focus on. Those two goals are the revenue of new sales that you need to meet your sales quota, or the number of new clients necessary to hit the same quota.

As you work on this part of the Focus Document, consider the time frame it's designed for. I suggest that you use it to set goals both for twelve months and three years. Most sales people over-commit to what they want to accomplish in one year and under-commit to what they will do in three years. Optimally, you want a goal here for both one year and three years.

Some corporations develop a mission statement that specifically addresses where they want to be ten, fifteen, or twenty years in the future. Salespeople don't think that way. Some salespeople choose a goal that will take three years to achieve and create a theme that helps them focus their energy on implementing the key strategies. Others might list a goal or goals just for the coming year. Use what you know about the person to help determine which type will work best for him or her.

Key Strategies

Once you've determined the goals, you can start determining the key strategies to implement. Here, you're looking for three to five major changes that the salesperson needs to make for significant growth of his business. Sure, small changes can add up, and I'll get to those in the tactic page as part of the Breakthrough Learning Document, but what you really want here are the major strategies that the salesperson has to implement to move forward.

Most of the major strategies generally fall into one of these ten areas:

1. Product knowledge
2. Sales process, especially fact-finding
3. System to get new clients
4. System to sell more to existing clients
5. Hiring staff or using current staff to do more administrative tasks
6. System to get more top clients
7. Intellectual capital necessary to add more value for clients
8. Joint-selling with other salespeople on their team
9. Developing relationships with individuals who can introduce them to top prospects
10. Joining organizations where they will meet top prospects

Most salespeople in the survival and stability phases should be able to easily identify several areas for improvement. If you have a salesperson in the stability or success phase who feels he's mastered these areas, here's another series of questions to identify appropriate strategies to implement:

1. What am I good at that I want to get great at?
2. What am I average at that I cannot delegate that I want to get good at?
3. What do I need to delegate?
4. What do I need to stop doing that makes me feel good but isn't important?
5. What do I need to find a better, faster, and easier way of doing?
6. What change have I been thinking of making, but haven't acted on?

Based on the answers to all the above questions, a salesperson should pick three to five areas for the "key strategies" section of the Focus Document. Depending on experience level, a salesperson may consider ten to sixteen different areas, but you can't successfully implement that many strategies at once!

That's why you help the salesperson choose about four core strategies that are most important in getting him to his goal. The faster he wants to progress in his career, the *fewer* strategies he needs to implement and the more frequently he will need to meet with you to focus his energy on implementing those strategies. If he wants to tackle more than that, tell him it's much more effective to focus his energy on just a few strategies than to spread himself too thin trying (and failing) to implement too many of them.

The strategies implemented will depend on the individual salesperson and where he is in his career. In phase one, which is primarily for new salespeople who have no experience in selling the product or service, the salesperson should focus on three things. The first, obviously, is product knowledge. Many sales coaches say, "You don't need to know anything about the product—we'll have other people to help you with that." Unfortunately, salespeople must know about the product to market it successfully.

The next key piece of learning for somebody in the first phase is an understanding of the entire sales process, especially the fact-finding process where they uncover clients' needs. So, the sales process begins with learning how to put people in your sales pipeline, how to call on them, how to schedule a first appointment, how to build trust, how to uncover needs, how to develop solutions, how to overcome objections, how to implement the new product or service, and how to stay in contact. That is a lot of knowledge to develop, but it's all lumped together in "understanding the sales process."

The third key element, and the single most important element for anybody starting out in sales, is developing a system to get new clients. If you don't have that system, your sales process, no matter how good you are, is irrelevant. You may be the go-to person on product knowledge, but with no one to meet with and sell to, you're out of luck. So out of these three things, the emphasis should be on creating a system to meet new people.

Now consider a salesperson in the stability stage. The key strategy for this person is to start upgrading his market. When you're in survival mode, you don't have to worry about upgrading your market—you've got to sell to anybody that's going to want to buy from you. Over time, however, you realize that you only have a limited amount of selling time and you need to upgrade your market and work with better customers.

The final key strategy is to determine how to get your administrative work done more effectively, either using the resources of your company or hiring your own staff to do the administrative tasks. Either way, you get more time back—time that can be spent actually selling.

Somebody currently in the success stage may still be working on the key elements from phase one and phase two, but now they have the luxury of adding three more key elements. One is the ability to bring tremendous value to the client. In other words, they need to have intellectual capital not only around their product, but how this product can be used more effectively within the person's organization. In the field of financial services, this value might be an understanding of tax law. For an engineered product, that value might be an understanding of how this product fits in with other engineered products, or maybe the value is a broad sense of more complex engineering.

The next skill salespeople should master in this stage is how to work effectively with a team of people. Even if the person has significant intellectual capital, many times because of the complexity of the sale, he'll have to work with other product experts or bring in additional team members.

The final thing for salespeople to do at this stage is to create relationships outside your organization that will benefit them. This includes belonging to associations and organizations related to their business. It might include joining a country club or industry group. The goal is to network with other professionals that sell similar products and services to the same clients that the salesperson does. This lets him trade referrals, and build additional relationships. This is a more advanced way of getting new clients.

Based on your experience, you as the sales coach can help the salesperson come up with major strategies that you know move people in your organization from one income level and one phase of their career to the next. Regardless of experience level, you help him come up with three to five major strategies that will take the person to the one-year goal and also help him reach the three-year goal. Keeping this in mind, while the strategies may need to be implemented now, it could be two or three years before you even see the payoff for them. Make sure that the person understands that the payoff may take some time!

Support

The last element on the Focus Document is support. Nobody is an island who can do things totally on his own. Some people like to think so, which brings me back to the idea of coachability. Coachable people are looking for support from other people because it accelerates growth. This person is willing to ask himself, "What do I need from others that will help me perform at my best?"

What every salesperson needs is someone who understands the challenging task of implementing these strategies, and someone who will give him positive feedback and recognition for the progress that he's making. Who will help him figure out solutions to complex problems that arise? Who will help him provide resources—money, equipment, and people—to get the job done? Who will challenge him to perform at his best even if things are not going well?

Hopefully, you are the person who will provide that support, but remember that often sales coaches are excellent at challenging people, but not as effective at analyzing people's self-defeating thinking or providing feedback. If you know you're great at creating drive, but not good at being a support to somebody or being a good teacher or shrink, then you're going to have to find the salesperson other people who can fill those roles.

In other words, get over the ego of being all things to the salesperson. You have to realize that you're not going to be the only one in the salesperson's life who can help her achieve her goals. As a young swim coach, I sometimes felt insecure when I saw one of my athletes relying on outside resources to

Sample Focus Document

PURPOSE — *What I do for others*
- Help clients come up with better solutions to their problems.

VALUE — *What separates me from other salespeople*
- Being creative and bringing needed ideas to clients.
- Challenge thinking to look at situations from multiple points of view.
- Make difficult problems easier to understand.

PAYOFF — *What I get as a result of achieving my purpose*
- Sense of fulfillment. Recognition. Better quality of life for my family.

NEEDS — *What I don't have enough of*
- I want to have more impact.

KEY GOALS — *What I must achieve that will give me what I need*
- A 20 percent increase in my client base.

KEY STRATEGIES — *How I will achieve my goals*
- System to upgrade my market.
- Networking at industry events.
- Increased knowledge on technology-advanced products.
- Better service team to allow me to prospect.

SUPPORT — *What I need from others so I can perform at my best*
- Regular coaching sessions to help me more effectively implement change.

improve. But over time, I realized that somebody who wants to achieve a goal may need more than just me to be successful. So even if you are an outstanding motivator, teacher and shrink, don't believe you're the *only* one who can help.

The purpose of the Focus Document is to give salespeople a clear direction of where they're going and how they are going to get there. It's a way of having the salesperson ask questions like the following: "What's really important to me? What separates me from other people? What am I doing for other individuals? What's the key goal that I have to achieve? How am I going to achieve the goal? And who are the people I'm going to call on to help me get to the goal?"

I suggest that when people finish their Focus Document, they type it out and frame it. It's a visual reminder of where they're heading, the strategies they're going to use to get there, and the people who can help them. The Focus Document provides clarity, and magnifies energy the way a magnifying glass does. Even people who have limited energy can maximize their resources by spending it on clear, attainable tasks. (In addition to the blank Focus Document in the Appendix, you'll find a completed Focus Document on the next page to give you an idea of what a finished one looks like.)

Once you've developed the Focus Document with the salesperson, what happens next?

Different people in different career stages will need different things. Some may need you to simply tell them what to do next. Some salespeople who are in the stability and success phases may have to go out and interview current clients to more clearly define their personal value to their clients. But now that the Focus Document is done, you want to take one of the key strategies and get the salesperson to start implementing it. That's where the Breakthrough Learning Document comes in.

The Breakthrough Learning Document

The Breakthrough Learning Document is at the heart of this book. (A completed Breakthrough Learning Document is on page 83 and a blank copy is in the Appendix, page 143.) It creates *drive* in the positive rewards and negative consequences section. It lets the salesperson examine *self-defeating thinking* and establish ways to overcome it. Finally, in the tactics section, the document helps identify *new learning* and new ways of *thinking*.

You work with the salesperson at this point to determine how many Breakthrough Learning Documents to develop. Some salespeople can work on multiple Breakthrough Learning Documents; others have more success implementing one at a time. Somebody in survival mode may only be able to handle one Breakthrough Learning Document at a time. And the most important one for someone new to sales is a system to get new clients.

So whether you have multiple Breakthrough Learning Documents or just one, the idea is to make the key strategy real and attainable. It's drilling down to be even more focused with the energy that is available to get the person to create change. So let's get started creating one of your own.

Focus Date

You begin at the top of the page, with the focus date. Nothing happens quickly and overnight with major strategies. It takes time; I suggest you give a major strategy three months to get implemented. So, at the top of the page, you'll want to record today's date and a date three months from now as the implementation date. If the person can do it more quickly than that, you move on to the next strategy. If it takes longer, so be it.

Key Strategy/Outcome

The key strategy is one of the strategies you identified in the Focus Document. The key strategy must be clear, and the "outcome" section should reflect an indication of successfully implementing the strategy. For instance, if a key strategy is to more effectively use staff, an outcome might be that the salesperson has X number of new appointments in the field than before, or that the salesperson is able to spend 80 percent of his time on new client acquisition. The point is that the strategy needs to be something that can be quantifiable and measurable in the key outcome.

Positive Rewards

The positive rewards need to focus back on what creates drive. Have the salesperson consider these questions: "If I accomplish and implement this strategy and I get the outcome that I want, what does that mean to me? Does it mean more money? Does it mean more recognition? Does it mean a feeling of accomplishment? Less stress?" Record the answers as concrete reminders of *why* the person is implementing this process.

Negative Consequences

Fear can be a powerful motivator *if* the negative consequences are something the salesperson really doesn't want to happen. What are the negative consequences that will result if the strategy is not implemented? In other words, what will happen if you don't make the change? Negative consequences aren't necessarily the opposite of what the person wants, but rather something the salesperson wants to avoid happening. For example, if you don't make this change, your sales territory will be cut, or you won't get the promotion you've been working for over the last year.

Self-Defeating Thinking

Here's the stage where you really have to put on your "shrink" hat as a sales coach. This area of self-defeating thinking is what takes energy away from the drive. It's the normal push-back resistance to change and it includes all of the bad attitudes that people have about change. But self-defeating thinking is normal, and part of change. It's also what keeps people from changing, and the only way you can solve the problem of resistance to change is by getting the self-defeating thinking out in the open.

When you consider where the salespeople are in their careers—survival, stability, or success—note that it's much easier for them to verbalize the self-defeating thinking the longer they have been in the career. One of the reasons for that is that they're more secure with who they are based on their success. So it's not unusual for a new salesperson in the survival stage to refuse to admit to his self-defeating thinking. You'll have to show him what your self-defeating thinking was when you were in the same situation, or even what some of your self-defeating thinking is currently as you think about implementing change yourself. This is a way to both demonstrate empathy and to gain respect as a leader.

There are four basic types of self-defeating thinking to explore here—current actions, new problems, negative feelings, and beliefs. Let's look at each type in turn.

First, what *current actions* will the salesperson need to stop doing or find a better way of doing to find the time to implement the strategies in the Breakthrough Learning Document? Usually, these things provide some kind of psychic payoff—otherwise, why do them? Eliminating the task, finding a faster way to get it done, or delegating it can all be addressed in the "tactics" section, discussed below.

For someone at the survival stage, this might include things like micromanaging a sale or spending too much time talking to the prospect or client when it's clear the prospect doesn't want all that contact. A more established salesperson might have to stop working with low-priority clients. While that may give her a sense of security or a feeling that she's doing good work, it doesn't increase productivity. Or she might have to stop helping people in other departments. That may provide psychic income and warm feelings, but it doesn't help the salesperson achieve her particular goal. And even a successful salesperson may be spending too much time networking, which gets in the way of implementing the major breakthrough that they have identified.

There are also things that the salesperson may have to find a faster, smarter way of doing. She may have to delegate some tasks to an administrative assistant, and stop doing things like case proposals, order entry, routine client service, or chasing service work requests.

What *new problems* will the salesperson encounter as he implements the breakthrough strategy? These are the fears he has as he starts to work on the Breakthrough Learning Document. The positive rewards for implementing the breakthrough are in the future, while the problems are now. This gets us into the area of fear—"If I make the change, I'm going to encounter a new problem that I don't want to face." For example, if a salesperson starts upgrading her market, a new problem may be that she experiences an immediate drop-off in sales. The salesperson might go backwards. If she implements a new team-selling strategy, consider the potential problem if the client doesn't like the person she's doing team-selling with. The salesperson could lose the relationship.

These problems are always fear-based. The problem, or possible problem, is something the salesperson thinks is going to happen. Even if it doesn't happen, the potential of a problem may be very real in the person's mind, and as a result, she won't want to take the chance of implementing the strategy. The key strategies in the Breakthrough Learning Document should really push her to make a change.

What *negative feelings* does the salesperson have as he thinks about implementing this plan? Negative feelings are normal, but, unfortunately they lead to negative thinking, which leads to a lack of action. Developing new ways of thinking that will give the salesperson more positive feelings are part of the tactic section, and will lead to being more proactive in implementing the Breakthrough Learning Document.

Let's look at some of these negative feelings. The salesperson in the survival stage may feel like he is being pushy as he implements the change of improving the sales process. By asking questions of potential clients, he may feel like he's prying into the other person's life. If he's implementing a strategy to meet new people and ask for referrals, he might feel like a beggar. If the person is moving from stability into success and upgrading his market, he might feel that he's inadequate because he doesn't know how to deal with someone who has a lot more authority and status than he does. These are normal feelings. In fact, feelings are always normal, but the thinking behind those feelings could be totally irrational. As you move to the tactic page, you'll see what the new thinking needs to be to overcome these negative feelings.

What *beliefs* might prevent implementing the Breakthrough Learning Document? After all, this new strategy may conflict with the salesperson's beliefs that got her where she is now. Does she believe that doing her job differently will really work? Examples of these beliefs include: "I don't think that working on my knowledge is a good use of my time." "I don't believe that my number one problem for growing my business is identifying and getting new clients." "I don't believe that a sales assistant will ever be as smart as I am in solving problems." "I don't believe that the market that I'm in will allow me to achieve my goals."

Keep in mind that the person may have all kinds of negative reasons for not wanting to implement the change; as a result, she can build a powerful case against it. Recall that in Chapter Two, I suggested that when somebody talks about a belief, you need to ask, "Where did that belief come from?" When we get to tactics in a bit, you'll learn how to help the person come up with new beliefs that will help put the old beliefs behind him.

You can serve as a valuable resource by assisting the salesperson to answer the self-defeating thinking questions. Some people don't want to look at this part of their personality, so don't be afraid to be open with your own struggles in this area. When you share what you've encountered when facing these issues, the salesperson can feel comfortable in being vulnerable because ultimately that vulnerability leads to success.

Tactics

Finally, the salesperson must decide what she needs to do to implement the Breakthrough Learning Document and minimize self-defeating thinking. These tactics are the action plans to make the strategies addressed in the Focus Document real. Maybe the person you're coaching needs to learn new skills. Maybe he needs to acquire new knowledge, or needs to learn how to plan, use staff, or implement new marketing procedures. Or he has to figure out where he is going to get money for a budget item, or if he's self-employed, he might have to go out and get a line of credit.

Consider:

1. *Skills*: Does the person need to learn how to do certain things—such as how to effectively close a sale or make an initial sales call?
2. *Knowledge*: Does the salesperson lack the requisite information or data he needs to sell? For example, does he know how his product stacks up against the competition, and what benefits it provides to people who use it?
3. *Habits*: The salesperson may have to change habits that are negatively impacting her success, or create new habits—such as making calls at certain times of the day—that will increase her productivity.
4. *Staff*: How does the person work with staff at his company? Are there resources available at the company that he's not using? If he's self-employed, does he need to hire someone to take care of administrative tasks, freeing him up for more client contact time?
5. *Marketing procedures*: The salesperson may need to take a new approach to how he actually sells, or fine-tune his current approach to attract more business.
6. *Operational procedures*: For example, does the salesperson not know how to use the new order entry process or the most efficient way to bill clients?
7. *Technology usage*: Harnessing the appropriate technology can save a salesperson a tremendous amount of time, but he may have avoided or neglected learning which tools can help him work more efficiently.
8. *Financial issues*: For example, does the salesperson have enough in her budget to achieve her goals? If not, how does she ask for additional money from the company?
9. *New beliefs*: The classic example is someone who doesn't see himself as a salesperson; this will have to be replaced by a belief in his own selling ability to become successful. Or the salesperson may believe that his market is limited, or that people won't want his product. In addition to offering your own experience, you might suggest the salesperson ask his peers about times when they overcame negative beliefs or replaced them with more positive ones.
10. *New thinking*: New thinking is an essential element of incorporating

all of the above tactics, but it may also be as simple as helping someone who has a hard time hearing the word "no." Here, you could teach the salesperson the phrase, "Some will, some won't—move on." (Because new beliefs and new thinking are so complex, you'll find more techniques about overcoming negative feelings and beliefs in Chapter Six.)

Score Card

The outcome section at the beginning of the Breakthrough Learning Document is one measurement that indicates progress toward successful implementation of the strategy. You and the salesperson should now work together to establish three other key measurements that indicate progress in the "Score Card" section.

These key measurements are things that you or your salesperson will track in addition to measuring the sales results you're seeking. Measurement improves performance, so the key measurements provide more than only one outcome to determine whether progress toward the one and three year goals is being made. You might track the number of sales calls made. You might track the amount of time the salesperson spends on the phone, or how much time he spends studying. Or you can track how much the salesperson has in open case inventory in your sales pipeline, or how many times the salesperson is meeting with centers of influence that can help him build his market. (See the following page for an example of a completed Breakthrough Learning Document.)

Remember that a new salesperson in the survival stage is going to need to be told what these are. A person who's in the stability or success stage may already know them, but it doesn't hurt to remind him of these key measurements.

Sample Breakthrough Document

FOCUS: January to April

KEY STRATEGY OUTCOME

Pick one of the key strategies from the Focus Document

- Better service team

What would be the expected results after three months of working on the key strategy?

- Team identified and handled 80 percent of service calls

POSITIVE REWARDS

What are the positive rewards for implementing the breakthrough?

- New clients
- Raise
- Bonus
- New learning

NEGATIVE CONSEQUENCES

What are the negative consequences if the breakthrough isn't implemented?

- Stuck with mundane tasks

continued on next page

SELF-DEFEATING THINKING

What will you need to stop doing or find a better way of doing to find time for implementing the breakthrough?

- Talking so much with clients I like

What new problems might you encounter as you implement the breakthrough?

- Client complaints
- Mistakes and lost clients

What feelings do you have when thinking about implementing the breakthrough?

- Nervous that administrative team won't learn fast enough
- Scared

What belief might prevent implementation of the breakthrough?

- I have built my business on service—now someone else will be delivering the promise

continued on next page

TACTICS

What will I do differently to implement the breakthrough and minimize self-defeating thinking?

Consider:

Skills: Knowledge:

- What to tell clients about my service system
- Educate staff person on change in contact frequency

Habits: Staff:

- Regular meetings with staff person
- Ask for a dedicated staff person who reports to me

Marketing Procedures: Operational Procedures:

- Develop A-B-C service levels

Technology Usage: Financial Issues:

- Service notes in data base

New Beliefs: New Thinking:

- Clients will get better service from my team than I can give
- My team wants to learn as much as I do

continued on next page

SCORE CARD

What are the key measurements to review monthly that indicate your business is growing?

Sales results

New first appointments with new prospects

Open inventory of business pending

From Focus to Tactics

In this chapter, you've learned about the different stages that salespeople move through. Regardless of the stage they're in, the Focus Document and the Breakthrough Learning Document can create energy and spur them to meet their goals. You might not need to walk through and complete a Breakthrough Learning Document for a highly motivated, successful salesperson. But using this general process to get him to commit to a new goal can provide additional insight about what he needs to do to implement the change and what new learning he needs to grow his business. Bottom line? Whether or not you choose to go through these tools step by step, you should use the basic format and content of these tools because they address the key concepts of drive, new learning and self-defeating thinking.

The Breakthrough Learning Document interrelates with the Growth-Rate Formula, or GRF, because positive rewards and negative consequences impact drive. The new learning is addressed in the tactic section, and the self-defeating thinking is identified while new ways of thinking and new beliefs overcome it. Using the documents discussed in this chapter will help you increase the energy and focus of the people you coach. And as a sales coach, that is your role—to help them focus that energy on a few key things that will have significant impact on their careers.

5

The Coaching Process

Key concept: Relationships are built by helping people deal with anxiety.

At this point, you have the Focus Document and Breakthrough Learning Document(s) completed. The next step is to hold regular coaching review sessions to implement the Breakthrough Learning Document as quickly as possible.

The coaching review process includes three parts:

1. Educating the salesperson about the dynamics of anxiety and how to minimize it;
2. Assessing the quality of the relationship between you and the salesperson, and if necessary, addressing problems before the coaching review session begins; and
3. Using the coaching review session to address problems, brainstorm solutions, and accomplish mutual goals.

Understanding Anxiety

Let's take a look at the three major concepts that enable salespeople to minimize the normal anxiety that accompanies new learning and pursuing challenging goals. Without an understanding of these concepts, most salespeople may not be open or willing to discuss what needs to be done to improve performance.

Patience to Suspend Judgment

The number one barrier to communication is being judgmental, so as a sales coach, you must be able to suspend judgment while maintaining an open, inquiring mind. You want to create an atmosphere where the person you're working with feels safe and understood. As a coach, your role is the same as that of a counselor—when you listen and ask the right questions, you create an environment where the person feels secure and can tell you what he's thinking and feeling.

If you are judgmental, people won't feel safe revealing their thoughts and feelings with you. Anytime you make a judgment, regardless of whether the person's performance is good or bad, you're creating a barrier to open communication. Suppose you say something like, "That was great that you accomplished that goal!" to a salesperson. You think you're being positive, but you've still made a judgment—namely, that achieving that goal was great. And if you say something like, "Boy, that must have been awful," you're again making a judgment.

It's natural to make these judgments, but you can break the habit. It's as simple as asking someone, "How did that make you feel?" or "What were you thinking about this accomplishment?" Keeping the focus on the person's reaction (not your own) to an event eliminates the judgment.

Many people have a biased view about what therapy or counseling is. They think people go to counseling or are in therapy because "there's something wrong with them." The perception is that they must be sick or "goofy." The reality is that for most people, therapy is a coping strategy. It helps you learn how to cope more effectively with the realities of life.

People with this biased view (who typically have never been to a therapist) also tend to discount the process, claiming that therapists never really say anything—that "they just sit back and listen and let the patient talk." Guess what? That's the whole idea. A good therapist makes his patient feel safe. He does this by encouraging his client to talk openly, making her feel comfortable, and avoiding reacting, or judging her, through his words or actions. In fact, the therapist's body language should say, "I'm just listening and I want to learn about your situation." This is how you build trust with someone.

Salespeople know how critical trust is at each phase of the sales process. When you first meet someone, the person has to feel comfortable to talk about his situation and what his needs are. When you present a solution to his problem, does he trust that you're presenting a solution that is in his best interest? What if he's in no hurry to make a decision about the solution, or if he's anxious about what could go wrong when the solution is implemented? Trust is again an essential factor as you work through objections and implement the solution. This trust must be present in the coaching process as well.

I learned how to suspend judgment by working with my coach, Charles Betts, MD, the psychiatrist from Little Rock, Arkansas. We'd role-play coaching situations so I could determine what my strengths and weaknesses were. For example, I'd ask a question, and if I didn't hear an answer right away, I would show my lack of patience by starting to answer the question for him, rather than waiting to see what he'd say. In a way, that's a judgment. I'm judging the person as being unable to solve his problem. There must be something wrong with him.

From Dr. Betts, I learned about the concept of the power of silence, and how silence can help build a relationship where the person feels safe talking with you. I also improved my communication skills. We talked about situations that made me anxious or where I didn't know how to respond, and how that felt. I learned about myself in the process, and that can be a scary prospect.

If being judgmental is the number one barrier to communication, you must consider whether you're able to suspend judgment about your *own* behavior. That's usually a tall order. We judge ourselves everyday and when we do, we usually don't want to explore the problem that is causing us to act and feel the way we do. If you don't have someone who's helping you deal with your own fears, doubts, and anxieties, you're not going to be able to do it for others. But if you're able to disclose the way you think and feel to another person—without being judged for it—you can determine the nature of the problem, and learn more about yourself. That's why I worked with Dr. Betts—I believe that every good coach needs his own coach as well.

It's a great feeling to know that you can sit down with somebody and share what you're working on to talk through a problem and come up with a solution in a safe manner. That's what you're striving for here. You want the salesperson to understand that you're there to help, not judge.

Anxiety's True Source

Once you communicate the idea that judgment is the biggest barrier to communication, then you can explain the next key concept. That is: *anxiety is lack of mastery, not personal inadequacy.* Anxiety is just part of life. It's a normal consequence whenever anyone begins to learn something new.

Imagine putting your pen in your opposite hand and trying to write with it. It feels awkward. But instead of realizing it feels awkward because it's new, our usual response is something like, "What's wrong with me?" or "I can't believe this feels so hard," or "I can't believe I'm feeling this way."

The reality is that there is nothing wrong with you. You just haven't accepted the concept that *anxiety is a lack of mastery, not personal inadequacy.* Take exercising. Working out often produces physical pain or soreness. I accept it as a normal consequence of getting in shape, and realize that stressing my body beyond its usual limits is going to cause pain. But as my fitness level improves, the physical pain for the same level of effort is less.

The same theory is true for learning anything new. At first, the salesperson experiences emotional pain, rather than muscular pain or soreness, when she attempts something new. She needs to look at the pain as normal, not as a sign that there is something wrong with her. As her learning improves, this emotional pain lessens.

The question is, what is the salesperson trying to learn? Obviously she's trying to master a new way of doing something. That's learning new skills. But there's something else as well—the self-talk that accompanies trying to do something new. To master and overcome negative beliefs that create anxiety, you must overcome negative *feelings* that create anxiety, and the thinking that those feelings produce. That means embracing a new way of thinking about how you experience things—in other words, accepting that *anxiety is a lack of mastery, not personal inadequacy*, and making sure the salesperson realizes this!

Difference between Performance Self and Emotional Self

The third key concept that you should get across to build relationships with people is educating salespeople about the difference between the performance self and the emotional self. It's unfortunate that the only time a salesperson gets recognition is when he is performing well. That's what the performance self is all about. It's what people see. The performance self is the skills, abilities, and knowledge that lead to overall results when someone is performing at his best.

People see this and make positive comments about the behavior. But, unfortunately, it's easy for the salesperson to conclude that she's only a worthwhile human being when she is performing well. When a salesperson can't separate the performance self from the emotional self—her worth as a human being—she is not open to feedback because she takes it as a personal attack.

The emotional self is defined as "How I feel about myself." When the salesperson isn't performing well and starts taking this lack of performance as a sign that there's something wrong with her as a human being, she becomes anxious and responds defensively. That means she'll either run away or fight the problem. Most of us tend to want to run away instead of talking about the performance and learning what caused the poor performance. We don't want to know why we didn't perform well because we make the faulty assumption that it's going to come back to something that's wrong about us.

Keep in mind when you're giving feedback to a salesperson that it's natural for him to interpret it as "What's wrong with me," instead of "What's wrong with the performance." Or, he may get angry at you for giving performance feedback, and say something like, "You don't understand." "You're not helping me." "How come you can't give me some positive strokes?" "Why are you always critical?"

Understand that the reason he's fighting you is because he's taking your feedback as a criticism of *him,* rather than his *performance.* Nearly everyone is confused about the difference between the performance self and the emotional self because of the way that we were raised. This isn't an attack on parents who thought they were doing the right thing by complimenting us for doing well on a test, or for performing well on the softball field or concert. This positive feedback as a child was interpreted as love.

One of my clients told me that he was driving home from his twelve-year-old son's hockey game. His son hadn't played well, and my client wasn't saying anything to him. Suddenly his son blurted, "Dad, how come you only like me when I play well?"

This is where the concept of the performance self/emotional self is learned. As parents, we want our children to do their very best. When they don't, we turn into their coaches. We start telling them how they can get better. However—and I had to learn this with my own daughter—we should let the coaches and teachers do that. As parents, we have to show our children that we love them for who they are regardless of what happens. When they come off the playing field, we should treat them the same whether they perform well or they perform poorly.

Yet this was a difficult thing for me to learn as a parent because, as a coach, I was always giving feedback. As a coach, your role is to challenge. As a parent, you can still challenge your children, but not at the moment of their performance. You have to wait for a more opportune time.

Remember, many of us—probably most of us—grew up in environments where the only time we got recognition was when we were performing well. We may not have learned that who we are as human beings had nothing to do with performance and that we were loved, appreciated, and cared for regardless of how we performed.

When a salesperson is aware of this difference or distinction between the performance self and the emotional self, she realizes that any negative feedback from the coach is directed at her behavior, not her worth as a human being. As a result, you don't create relationship tension that makes problem-solving difficult. You eliminate this tension. This concept must be shared if you are going to have any type of relationship with the individuals that you're coaching.

Assessing the Relationship

Once you've shared these concepts with the person you're working with, you need to assess the quality of the relationship you have together. There are two ways to do this. First, you can simply ask the person to rate the relationship on a scale of 1 to 10, with 1 being "horrible" and 10 being "great." If this number is lower than you'd like, ask the salesperson what needs to happen to improve it.

You can also assess the relationship in a more subtle way, and without asking the salesperson to evaluate it. Simply examine the level of communication you have with the person—this will tell you how strong (or weak) the relationship is.

As you deepen the level of communication, you build stronger, better relationships with the people you work with. In short, the higher the level of communication you have, the more comfortable a salesperson feels and the more revealing and open he will be with you.

To determine the level of communication, listen to what the salesperson is saying as the two of you talk. There are generally four levels of communication that you use when you're talking to someone. The higher the level of communication the salesperson uses, the more trust he has in you. The four levels include:

Cliché Level

This is the most basic level of communication. It's the way that we usually open communication with people. It's "How's the weather?" "What's going on with your favorite team?" "What's happening in the news?"

This is safe because neither person is sharing much about himself or herself. This type of communication is designed to break the ice. If you know you're going to have to get into a difficult conversation, you don't jump right into the hot topic. You table the issue until you've moved past the ice-breaking stage.

Factual Level

The next level of conversation involves just facts. Facts look like this: "Tell me what's going on. Tell me the good, the bad, and the ugly about what's going on in your world. I want to know." Typically when asked, the salesperson will share facts with us.

Facts are safe. We know what they are. They're obvious from records and data that we keep. For example, we know what the market looks like, we know what the person's activity level is, and we know what the sales figures are. As you examine these facts, remember to suspend judgment—you don't know how the salesperson evaluates those facts.

Thinking Level

The next level of communication is the thinking level. In other words, you ask, "As you look at those facts, what are you thinking?" Looking at the facts, you might assume that a top salesperson is happy with spectacular sales results. But the salesperson might be thinking, "I'm not performing at the level that I want to—these numbers are good, but not good enough."

The same is possible as you look at the facts surrounding a poor performer. Here, you might ask, "What are you thinking?" and the salesperson might respond that everything's fine. She may actually be in denial about the facts. By asking what the person is thinking, you get a better perspective on her perception of reality without making a judgment.

Feelings Level

While getting someone to tell you what she's thinking is good, the highest level of conversation and the one that shows the most vulnerability is the feeling level of conversation, i.e., "How are you feeling about your situation?"

Let's go back to the top salesperson. In your mind he's getting great results, but in his, those results aren't as good as they could be. When you ask him what he's feeling, he says, "I'm feeling inadequate." Even though he's getting excellent results from your point of view, he doesn't think they're good. At a deeper level, he's feeling inadequate, so now you can get to the point of what the real issue is.

In this case, it's not the facts that are the problem—it's his feelings about himself. That's the problem you have to help him deal with—the emotional issue. Let's go back to the poor performer I mentioned. When you ask what she's thinking about her results, she says she has no problem. Asked about how she's feeling, she might say she's feeling confident. (Again, she may be in denial, and in the next chapter, you'll learn how to help people who are in denial.)

It's really difficult for people to express their feelings. In the Appendix, page 147, you'll find a long list of feelings ranging from "bummed" to "embarrassed" to "indignant." Some of my clients have laminated this document and use it when they're having this conversation with someone they're coaching. They hand it out and ask people to pick some of the feelings they're experiencing, and you may want to do the same thing.

Expressing feelings is the highest level of communication. If people are reluctant to be more open, you can share the thoughts and feelings you had when you faced similar situations. You may have to be vulnerable to make someone else feel safe, and the best way to do that is by sharing feelings that you've had. If the salesperson is doing something new, whether it's selling new products, or trying a new procedure, or going after a bigger goal, anxiety is normal and so are the feelings that accompany that anxiety. When you share your own feelings, you continue to build trust with the person you're coaching.

Addressing Tension

As you engage in conversations with salespeople, often you'll feel tension in the relationship. You might be getting facts from the person, but she's reluctant to have her thinking align with those facts. Or you're asking about her feelings and she doesn't want to share her feelings. She clams up, and you start to feel frustrated. You should address the frustration or relationship tension before you get into solving the problem. After all, how can you solve a problem if the person won't even put a problem on the table?

If you start telling somebody what to do and she hasn't even admitted she has a problem, you become too pushy. You become the dominant controlling parent and the overbearing, uncaring, unsympathetic sales coach. That's why this relationship tension must be addressed before you can move on.

Again, in the Appendix, page 148, there is a list of "personal frustration" questions to help get this topic out in the open. Something has happened in your relationship with the individual that's preventing her from opening up. Maybe you trigger emotions from the past when she had to deal with an authority figure, so even though she's sitting with you, you're not her sales coach anymore. Now you're the critical parent or the critical teacher she never got along with in the past, and she's projecting these past emotions onto you, which stops communication.

In psychology, this is called transference. People transfer onto the sales coach emotions about other people in their life they haven't been able to cope with. Until you can repair this tension, you may be viewed as uncaring, and you're never going to be as good of a coach as you could be to help them work on their performance.

The idea of the personal frustration questions is to get the person to stop talking about the problem and start talking more about your relationship. My favorite one to use is "I feel like we are battling now—do you feel the same way?" If the person says "yes," then you explore that, asking "What are we battling about?" This means the person has to give us feedback. It might have been something that you did or said that triggered a feeling in the person that you were not safe to talk to. If you give him permission to open up by saying something like, "Tell me what's on your mind," "Tell me what I need to know about you," or "Tell me about your reluctance to share what's really going on," you might receive personal criticism in return. This has to be addressed before you can get back to the performance problem.

Handling Personal Criticism

I suggest a four-step process for responding to these kinds of disparaging comments. The first step is to acknowledge the criticism by stating the emotion you see the person demonstrate. You might make comments like "You look frustrated." "I see that you are really angry." "You seem really upset with me." These statements lead to explanations which diffuse the anger.

By naming the emotion (the person can correct you if you're wrong), you show a sense of understanding for that emotion. Once you've acknowledged the emotion, you need to keep him talking. This is the second step. When someone blurts out a global statement like, "You are the worst coach I've ever worked with," you have to keep him talking until you get to a specific problem that can be addressed.

You do that by continuing to probe. "Well, tell me more about how you feel I'm a bad coach." The person may say, "You never listen," or "You're always telling me what to do," or "I'm feeling overwhelmed." Now you're drilling down from a broad statement like "You're the worst coach in the world" to a more definitive problem that can be addressed.

Next, agree with the statement by accepting responsibility that your behavior can negatively impact the salesperson's performance. Don't deny the mistake. You might say: "You know, you're right. I can be that way. I am challenging sometimes. I get frustrated at times." As you agree with the stated problem, don't give a reason for why you do what you do. The person doesn't care that you're pushing him because you're behind on quota and are feeling nervous. What he cares about is *how* he's being treated, not the reasons why he's being treated that way.

Apologize if necessary by saying something like, "You're right. I have been pushing you too hard and I apologize for it. I realize that it's now negatively impacting our relationship and I want us to have a more open dialogue here."

Finally, in step four, you ask for, or offer, a resolution to the problem, such as "How do we solve this?" "How would you like me to give you feedback on how you are doing?" Or "How would you like me to handle this in a more appropriate way so that I can help you achieve your goals?" By asking the person what he would like as the solution, he owns the solution. And he's telling you the best way to communicate with him as he moves forward.

What if the solution is off-base or doesn't work? Then you point that out, and tell the salesperson you still need to work toward a solution that makes him feel that you're not pushing too hard, but that addresses the reality of the situation, such as being behind on goals. You work toward a resolution that both of you can live with, and then you can get back to talking about the actual concept of resolving the conflict.

The Johari Window

As you're assessing the relationship, you should be aware of something that can dramatically impact it. It's a communication model that was developed by American psychologists Joseph Luft and Harry Ingham called the Johari Window. It addresses the four elements of communication; being aware of these four elements allows you to be more empathetic and understanding of how you may overpower someone or damage the relationship when you think you're being helpful.

	Known to self	Not known to self
Known to others	**Arena**	**Blind Spot**
Not known to others	**Façade**	**Unknown**

Johari Window

Let's look at how the Johari Window applies from a salesperson's perspective. Window number one is called Arena, and is common knowledge. It's something that you as my coach and I both know about myself. Because it's common knowledge, I feel safe talking about it. And if we both feel safe talking about it, we can resolve the problem.

Unfortunately, though, sometimes I don't feel safe, and the second window in the Johari Window is called Façade. These are my secrets, and I'm afraid to tell you my secrets because you might judge me. I'm afraid to tell you my secrets because I'll be vulnerable. I'm afraid to tell you my secrets because you might fire me. I don't trust you enough to be totally open and honest. When assessing relationship tension, you'll never get someone's secrets out in the open until the tension is gone and the person can be honest and vulnerable with you.

The third window is Blind Spots. Blind spots are things that the salesperson doesn't know but the coach does. You may be so tempted at times to say, "Here's what your problem is." But while you can be accurate in diagnosing the problem, whether it's that the salesperson is too aggressive or is a poor listener or has a hard time coping with bad news, if you don't have a good relationship with the individual and you tell him about a blind spot, he'll go into denial. It's likely that the revelation will also damage the relationship.

Sharing information about someone that he's never heard before can be overwhelming. People are often in therapy for a long time before any real progress is made, and the reason is that the therapist is trying to build the relationship to get the person to share his secrets. A smart therapist won't reveal an insight into his patient that the patient himself hasn't seen before because he may not be able to handle it. (Remember, this has happened to me—in Chapter Two, I shared how I drove a person to counseling because of the anxiety my comments produced in him.) Keep in mind that the relationship must be strong before you can start sharing someone's blind spot.

Finally, the fourth window is the called Unknown; for a sales coach/salesperson relationship, it represents the person's potential. From the salesperson's perspective, these are things about himself that he doesn't know and that you (the sales coach) don't know about him either. It's his untapped potential, his ability.

As the sales coach, how do you tap into this potential? You have to challenge the person to take on responsibility that he never thought he was capable of. You want to put him into challenging situations. But the people you're going to put into extremely challenging situations will be the people you have a great relationship with. They're the individuals who have shared their secrets with you. They're the ones who have been given information about their blind spots and worked through them. Now you're willing to put them into situations that neither you nor they know if they'll succeed at. This is the ultimate in getting into the untapped potential of salespeople, but it is an evolving process that takes time. Ultimately, though, it is all about the quality of the relationship that you have with the individual.

The Coaching Review Process

Now that you're aware of how your relationship with the salesperson can impact the quality of the Coaching Review process, the Coaching Review process actually becomes very straightforward and simple. A completed Coaching Review appears on the next page, so let's go through the points one by one.

What Is Going Well?

This is the first question to ask. I can't remember the number of times I've asked salespeople what's going well and they wind up telling me what's going

Sample Coaching Review

Continued growth is the result of drive and new learning minus the interference of self-defeating thinking that clutters the mind.

1. *What is going well?*
   - **Have had several clients buy additional products that at first they didn't think they needed.**

2. *What do you want to talk about?*
   - **Having difficulty with one of my top clients.**

3. *Rate your progress on your breakthrough on a scale of 1 to 7.*
   (1 is poor, 7 is exceptional)
   - **Rating is 5.**

4. *What needs to be done to improve rating?*
Consider:
   Drive — Look at your purpose, values, support, rewards and negative consequences.
   New learning — Look at your skills, knowledge and other tactics.
   Self-defeating thinking — Look at beliefs, new problems, negative feelings and rewarding activities that might need to be given up.
   - **I am finding it very difficult to let go of service work.**
   - **I want you to help me think through how to be a better delegator and what my thinking needs to be so I can let go.**

5. *Review Score Card.*
   - **All on track.**

6. *Commitments from last meeting and results.*
   - **I said I would meet more regularly with the new salespeople and I did.**

7. *On a scale of 1–7, with 1 being low, how helpful was this session? What would make it better?*
   - **Rating is 5. It would be better if you didn't seem so rushed.**

wrong. When things that are going well are shared, make sure the salesperson tells you what he did to get the favorable results. For individuals who have a difficult time discussing this, you may suggest that they keep a record of their accomplishments, including ones they made in the past or at previous positions they have held.

So you want the person to share what's going well and point out that a lot of good things have gone well—even little things. You want your salesperson to start thinking that he has the ability to have good things going on. Remember, when things have gone well, you don't gloss over it. You get the person to explain how that happened. That gets the salesperson to realize that good things don't happen by accident, and that their actions caused those positive outcomes.

What Do You Want to Talk About?

The next question is, what does the salesperson want to talk about? He feels in control when we ask him what he wants to talk about, and he's probably been thinking about it in advance, especially if he's been struggling with a problem. Once he shares his agenda, you can help him think through whatever it is he wants to talk about.

If the problem the salesperson brings up is of a personal nature, such as an illness, financial issue, or a family relationship, be aware that you might not have the time or ability to help him solve these problems. Tell the person you can understand how these issues can be very difficult and keep him from concentrating on work issues, but that you're not capable of being his counselor for problems unrelated to work. You may suggest that he finds an appropriate person—a therapist, doctor, or counselor—who can help him work through these problems.

While you can share if you've had a similar problem and how you solved it, you can't be the one who is responsible for solving personal problems. You're not the person's therapist, marriage counselor, or financial consultant. He has to find appropriate resources. You've learned already that you're not the only person in his world he can go to. You don't have the time to work on the personal problems that somebody might have (and they're way more complex than this book can address!).

Bring this issue back to work by saying, "I know it's difficult while you have these problems going on, but how do we balance your work performance with coping with these challenging outside influences?" You still want him to feel that he's in control and can bring up any problem that might affect the workplace. But you're only going to work with him on work-related problems; ones of a personal nature should be addressed by someone else.

What's the Progress on the Breakthrough Learning Document?

The salesperson comes to the coaching session with his own rating on the progress he thinks he's made on a scale of 1 to 7, with 7 being the best. You want self-diagnosis first—you're not judging the individual. He's judging his own performance. This self-diagnosis is a must if you are going to conduct a meaningful conversation. Many salespeople will be tougher on themselves than you as the sales coach could ever be.

What Needs to Be Done to Improve the Rating?

We'll talk about how we make progress on the Breakthrough Learning Document in the next chapter. In short, you want to be a motivator to help the person increase drive. You can be a teacher to help him learn new skills and knowledge and be successful, and you can be a shrink if what's getting in the way of progress is a problem of a self-defeating thinking nature. But before you get to that, the salesperson must first rate his progress and share it with you.

Score Card Review

You may or may not have to address these key measurements. If you both agree on the progress toward the Breakthrough Learning Document, you don't need to look at key measurements. But what if the salesperson thinks that progress on the breakthrough is a 7 and you think it's a 2? Then you can go back to the key measurements and ask for the facts that support his belief that he's progressing at a level of 7 toward the breakthrough.

Denial is one of the most difficult defense mechanisms to break through, and the only way you can break through to people who are in denial about their progress is to get them to examine the facts and to accept the facts. That's why key measurements are then necessary.

Unfortunately, too many sales coaches spend way too much time on the measurements. Don't get bogged down worrying about the numbers, which often provide nothing more than a blinding glimpse of the obvious. Measurements are diagnostic tools so that discussion can be directed to what can be done to improve them, whether it's an issue of drive, new learning, or self-defeating thinking.

What Were the Results of Commitments from the Previous Meeting?

This lets you determine whether the salesperson followed through with what he said he would do at the last meeting.

How Would You Rate Me as a Sales Coach?

This is an important question as it helps you know how effective you were in making this a great coaching session. Ask the salesperson to assess your rating. If it's poor, ask what you can do next meeting to make it better. And if it's good (or great!), say thank you.

Scheduling Coaching Sessions

There's one last consideration about this Coaching Review process and it depends on what level the salesperson is. The last factor to consider is how often you'll meet with the salesperson. In the last chapter, we talked about the three levels of the person's career—survival, stability, and success. When people are in survival mode, they have no choice. The frequency with which you meet with them will be up to you. However, if somebody is in the stability mode or the success mode, I always encourage sales coaches to ask three questions to determine appropriate meeting frequency. This again gives the salesperson the feeling of being in control, and that you're making them responsible for their own development.

The three questions are:

1. How often do you want to meet?
2. What length of time is best for you?
3. What would you like the agenda to be in these sessions?

You give them the option, but it's not solely up to them. The person in stability might only want to meet with you quarterly, but you as the coach might want to meet monthly. So you can discuss that, exploring why she only wants to meet once a quarter, and explaining why you think you should meet every month.

In addition, a person in the success mode who is making great progress in her career may not want to meet with you at all. You've got to be aware of this. This isn't a rejection of you; the person is just saying she's making tremendous progress and she doesn't want to be bogged down in an unproductive meeting. So don't be overbearing with somebody who's really successful.

If you see a successful person who's stuck or struggling, that's a different story. That might entail sharing with her the blind spot you see that is hurting her progress. Just be aware that if you share a blind spot with someone who hasn't accepted it, you run the risk of hurting the relationship.

I've found, however, that successful people who are stuck actually want to meet more frequently. And it's not necessarily about a lack of skills or new learning, but often because they don't have the next goal, or they don't feel the drive that they used to feel in their careers. A successful salesperson may need to go back and create an entirely new Focus Document to create a new sense of drive or to set new goals.

Recall that the documents that led to this Coaching Review session are the Focus Document, the one-page business plan, and the Breakthrough Learning Document. However, you can conduct the Coaching Review session without having the actual documents in front of you. Some people hate writing stuff down on paper. As long as the person's making progress and you both understand what's on each of these documents, you know the questions to ask based on your assessment of the person's progress. People in stability or success may not need completed Focus Documents or Breakthrough Learning Documents, but salespeople who are still in survival mode need to put all this information in writing. They need a lot more structure, but for some people structure can be overwhelming. That's why these documents are so simple.

Finally, I can't stress enough that the documents are irrelevant if you don't have a relationship with the individual. If she doesn't see you as being helpful to her, the documents are just words on a page. You must be sure that your salespeople can share facts, their thinking about those facts, and the feelings that those facts create with you. The relationship between the two of you is the essential element to make the coaching sessions as effective as possible.

6

Motivator, Teacher, Shrink

Key concept: Diagnosis is easy, prescription is difficult.

In the last chapter, you learned how to conduct a Coaching Review, and how to help your salespeople create solutions to implement their Breakthrough Learning Documents. While you've already learned how to respond to criticism from a salesperson, in this last chapter you'll learn more about the three primary roles you play as a coach—motivator, teacher, and shrink—and when to use each of them.

First, though, think back to the Growth-Rate Formula you learned about in Chapter One:

$$D + NL - 2(SDT) = \text{Growth Rate}$$

Remember, Drive ("D") creates the energy to learn new things (new learning, or "NL") while self-defeating thinking ("SDT") decreases the drive to make change. As a coach, you address the elements of drive, new learning, and self-defeating thinking with salespeople of all levels of experience. However, where a salesperson is in his career (survival, stability, or success) will affect what areas he needs to work on. A salesperson in survival mode may have an enormous amount of drive, but lack essential knowledge to achieve his goals. He may also be dealing with a lot of fear and other self-defeating thoughts and feelings that negate drive.

A salesperson in the stability mode has been around for a while, and probably understands more about self-defeating thinking than her peer who's just start-ing out. She's likely to be comfortable, so here your job as coach is figuring out how to push her beyond her comfort zone. That may mean assessing the new learning she needs to master, or dealing with ways to create new drive to make her want to move to the next level. The key exercise with someone at this stage of her career is the one that addresses resistance to change—these salespeople know they want more, but they also feel fine where they are and don't want to shake things up.

And for a salesperson in success, much of your discussion may be focused around drive—namely, how to create it when she's already at the top of her game. She already has a history of successfully making change to rise to the level where she's at, and may not need a lot of new learning. She just doesn't know what's next.

The Coach as Motivator

When people think of outstanding coaches, they often think of outstand-ing motivators. Yet the fact is that neither you, nor anyone else, can motivate another person. He has to motivate himself. However, as a sales coach, you can create an environment that helps people motivate themselves. When you sit down with someone one-on-one for a coaching session, you help create this kind of environment. The questions you ask, the feelings you share, and the way you listen can all help that person create internal drive.

Remember the five elements that create drive that we talked about in Chapter One? They are recognition, impact, a sense of belonging, mastery, and money. All of the strategies that you use to create drive should address one or more of those issues. The strategies you use will vary, but here are effective ones to consider:

Recognition

I spoke at a world sales meeting several years ago where many of the salespeople who had sold enough to attend had brought their spouses with them. At dinner, I asked a German salesman next to me what had created the drive to be there. His answer was; "It was easy! I had a picture of this resort up at home. My wife had never been outside of Germany and when she saw a picture of the resort, she decided she really wanted to go there. In the morning, when the alarm went off and I was deciding whether to stay in bed, my wife would put her foot in my back and say, 'Get out of bed so that we can win that trip to the Four Seasons Resort on Nevis!'"

In this case, the salesman wanted to please his wife; in the process, he received recognition from her, and others as well. This is a great example of how having a picture of the reward for achieving the goal can focus energy and remind someone of what he's working for. If your company has a newsletter, use it to recognize salespeople regularly. You can include information about sales quotas that were met, salespeople who brought in new customers, and those who received additional training or designations. In addition, you can include success stories of customers who have been helped, or any other information that provides recognition for individual salespeople.

Impact

The customer success stories I mentioned are an excellent way to show how salespeople make a difference in the lives of their clients. Another simple way to create drive around impact is to have salespeople ask their customers at the end of every appointment what the benefit has been of their spending time together. This gives the salesperson immediate feedback on his impact. Tell salespeople that they may never know the impact they have on the customers they serve—unless they ask.

Sense of Belonging

If you have salespeople who are motivated by a sense of belonging, consider holding fun activities for your sales team. This can be any activity that people enjoy—the whole idea is to get together as a group. You can tie this in with a contest; the prize might include a trip to a fun destination where people can participate in a variety of recreational activities (golf, sailing, skiing, shopping, you name it) that they enjoy. Being part of some type of event can have a dramatic impact on motivation for people who find it important to feel part of a group.

Realizing this, many companies are now holding "study groups," where salespeople get together regularly to talk about what they're doing. They can also use the group to ask for input from their peers on problems, or for feedback on the progress they're making on their individual Breakthrough Learning Documents. Having one-on-one coaching sessions are helpful, but reporting on your progress to a group provides both greater recognition and a sense of belonging. The group members can recognize new learning, producing a sense of mastery, and help salespeople appreciate their impact on customers as well.

Mastery

Outside speakers are another way to stimulate motivation, especially for those who are driven by mastery. The speaker may be an individual who has accomplished something you'd like your salespeople to achieve, who can address how he was able to make progress toward his goal, what obstacles he encountered, and how he overcame those obstacles. A speaker like this also gives your team a template or model to follow. Many people cannot create something new by themselves, but if they see how somebody else has done something, they can emulate that person and say, "If he can do it, then I can do it."

Money

Contests with financial incentives can motivate salespeople to make more money, and your company's compensation plan should address the monetary aspect of drive as well. While that may be obvious, an effective compensation structure should motivate salespeople to achieve both their individual goals, as well as the overall goals of the team or company.

While these types of activities will help create an environment that stimulates your salespeople and helps them achieve their unmet needs, nothing can replace the regular sessions where you review the progress on the Breakthrough Learning Document. The agenda for those coaching sessions incorporates the concept of motivation. You start the meeting with what's going well, and you get the person to talk about his successes so you can recognize him for it. He puts the problems he wants to solve on the table, making him responsible for them, with you acting as a resource, helping him identify progress and what he might do to continue to learn and grow.

In these meetings, you challenge people to focus on what's important and to look at the reality of their current situation so that collectively you can do something to change the progress they are making. That might mean using the Balanced Goal Exercise again to clarify what the person wants to achieve and why it's important to him. You can revisit the Focus Document, or go over the Breakthrough Learning Document and review the rewards and negative consequences that can increase drive. You can also use the Drive Exercise, which also appears in the Appendix, page 150, to help the salesperson identify what created drive in the past and figure out what will now create drive in the present.

Creating drive is the most difficult task a sales coach has because drive is an internal issue. Why do some people want to climb mountains? Why do some people enjoy playing golf? Why do some individuals want to be top salespeople, and others just want simple, uncomplicated lives and work toward that? The reasons are all internal and individual, and you may never understand why a person may be driven by one thing and not by another. But it's not necessary for you to know this. Your job is to help determine a goal that the salesperson wants to achieve. Identifying that goal will create energy—and that energy, when focused on the goal, creates drive to learn new things.

The Coach as Teacher

The second role that you play as a sales coach is that of a teacher. Not all successful teachers are great coaches, but all successful coaches are great teachers. If you think back to outstanding coaches you've had in sports, music, theater, or dance, you probably remember the amount of time that they spent getting you to master the fundamentals. "Practice makes perfect." Great coaches have you practice for hours for relatively short performances. In sales, unfortunately, you do a lot of performing but very little practice.

Here's the thing—no amount of drive can replace skill or ability. You might be driven to work long hours, but if your skills are poor, your performance will be, too. I might be driven to be a stellar golfer and really enjoy playing golf and get a lot of personal satisfaction out of it, but if you were to look at my golf swing, you wouldn't want me on your team. I'd need to learn a lot before I could be great, much less stellar, on the golf course.

But as a coach, how do you create the desire in someone to want to learn—and help them learn more quickly? By using the following four-step process:

1. First, you make sure that people *want* to learn. You do this by demonstrating the value, or payoff, of the learning—namely, how the learning will help them achieve the goal that's creating drive.
2. You present concepts in an understandable manner.
3. You test people to see if they know how to use the concepts. This may include role-playing so people can practice the learning before they implement it in sales situations.
4. You get people to use the concepts and learning immediately.

Here's an example so you can see how the process works. I've taught a one-day public speaking course that's effective for several reasons. As part of the introduction, I show videos of former attendees speaking both before and after they took the class. The people there realize very quickly that if they implement the skills they learn, they'll see tremendous results, so I have their attention. This is the law of readiness—people learn more quickly when what they're learning can immediately benefit them.

Second, I also make the course simple. There are only a few learning points that people can easily remember and start implementing. After teaching the key learning points, I test the attendees to see if they understand them. For the knowledge part of a presentation, they do paper and pencil exercises, but to test skills, the participants role-play. They're filmed doing the role-playing exercises after each key point taught, and then they are shown the tapes.

Third, as with any new learning, I ask them to self-diagnose their performance first, as well as express any anxiety they have trying something new, or being video-taped. By doing the role-play and watching it on tape, they can see themselves improving, which accelerates learning. Then I give them a final test—I show the video of their first and last presentations. They can see how much progress they've made, which gives them confidence to go out and use the skills they've learned. In fact, I ask them to use the skills in a presentation within a week so they don't lose it. That's the final step of the teaching process.

This may sound simple, but in most of corporate America, this is not the way that learning takes place. Most of corporate America is an information dump. Speakers and presenters tend to give people an awful lot of information, and they often say, "If you get just one great idea out of this session, it's worth it." This may be true, but when you overwhelm people with information, you don't give them a chance to actually integrate it and figure out how they're going to use it.

Second, many companies will send all of their salespeople to a workshop on the same topic, even though many of them aren't interested in the content. A more effective way is to ask your salespeople what they want to learn related to accomplishing their goals, and then send them to workshops that they are interested in.

The other problem is that information is often presented in a compressed time because many sales leaders don't want their salespeople out of the field. So a speaker may be asked to present a three-day program in just one day—i.e., "Let's just give them the meat of the course." Unfortunately, what's left out of the course is the role-playing or practice to let people get comfortable using the skills so they can more easily implement them after the course is over.

So, how can we solve these problems? As I mentioned, encourage salespeople to choose courses they're interested in, and let them take them with your approval. The important thing is that they have a chance to practice and implement the knowledge they learn. If the person delivering the course has follow-up exercises, the salesperson can use those, or you can have coaching sessions where you review the content of the learning and integrate that into the session.

Again, not all successful teachers are great coaches, but all successful coaches are great teachers because the coach has to be able to teach the skills salespeople need to have. As the coach, you should have any skill you're asking the salesperson to learn and demonstrate so you can role-play and practice the skill during coaching sessions.

The Coach as Shrink

I mentioned earlier that drive is the most difficult thing to create for an individual because what drives someone is personal and individual. Being a teacher is actually the easiest role to play of the three because you can teach skills, and you can test that the person has the skills or the knowledge. But what happens when the person doesn't use the new skills or knowledge because he's afraid to? Now we get into the concept of being the psychologist, or shrink.

There's a lot of misunderstanding about what psychologists do. Essentially, their role is to help people change the self-defeating thinking that is preventing them from either thinking bigger or implementing new behavior. As a sales coach, you are not trained to deal with issues of depression, drug or alcohol abuse, post-traumatic stress syndrome, or other issues that a professional psychologist would handle. You can, however, help the salesperson who you coach to think differently so she can more effectively handle the normal anxiety that goes with change and growth.

Before we look at how to change thinking, let's explore self-defeating thinking and where it comes from. The following are the four areas that can create self-defeating thinking (though they can also create positive thinking): genetics, environment, experiences, and thinking.

Genetics are the factors you're born with that can help or limit the accomplishment of future goals. If your hand-eye coordination is weak, you won't be a professional golfer. You won't play NFL football as a defensive lineman if you weigh 150 pounds. You won't be an opera star if you weren't born with strong vocal cords. Even though you can always improve, genetics are certainly a limiting factor in some areas of performance.

Environment is the second element, and its impact may be positive or negative. Your environment growing up could have made you feel good about yourself, given you a positive outlook on life, and made you believe you could accomplish anything. Or you could have been brought up in an environment where the message was, "What's wrong with you?" or "Can't you do anything right?" A negative environment like this one may cause you to doubt that you can ever get better, years or even decades later.

The third element that creates you is the sum of your own experiences. If you've had a tremendous disappointment, you might say, "I never want to experience that feeling again, so I won't take the risk of making change." Another person might have the same experience and respond by deciding that nothing is going to get in the way of achieving his goals, so experiences once again can be positive or negative.

We can't control our genetics, environment, or experiences, but we can control our thinking. Henry Ford said, "Think you can or think you can't—either way, you're right." Our thinking controls whether we are going to be able to learn new things. If you say to yourself, I'm capable of learning, you're going to learn. If you say to yourself, I can overcome any obstacle; you'll take the time to overcome them.

Sharing this with your salespeople will help them want to change the thinking that's holding them back. By using the exercises in the Appendix to ask specific questions, you'll assist the salesperson to become aware of self-defeating thinking. The salesperson should answer the question aloud—this helps her realize when her thinking is irrational. The following exercises help the salesperson to share her thoughts and feelings with you to begin implementing new learning or to think bigger. You'll find all of these exercises in the Appendix.

Resistance to Change

The first exercise, Resistance to Change, found on page 152, is one you use with someone who's in the stability or success stage of career. (New salespeople in survival mode are dealing more with fear, or worry, which I'll address next.)

Take a salesperson who knows he has to start cross-selling other product lines, but he's resisting the change. If you ask him what he's afraid will happen if he makes the change, he may say he'll look foolish (because he doesn't know enough about the new product), or that his sales will go down. His ego or identity may suffer, and if he's selling a broader set of products, he may not spend as much time with the manufacturer of the products he's selling, which may impact his relationship with that person.

As you continue with the exercise, you ask him how the change will impact others. He may tell you that current customers may be ticked off that he's not spending enough time with them. As far as his values and beliefs go, he may prefer to be an expert in one area, rather than a generalist in many. When asked about his feelings, he may tell you he's nervous. Finally, you ask him what his plan is to minimize his resistance and make the change. For example, he might decide to learn as much as he can about the new product, and first approach the clients with whom he has the best relationship with—and with whom he isn't afraid to make a mistake.

Worry

The next exercise to use with people, which is found on page 153, is helping them deal with worry. Worry, or anxiety, is normal when you're dealing with risk. People take three types of risk—physical, financial, and psychological. Physical risks include things like climbing mountains, sky-diving, motorcycle riding, or playing sports with a high chance of injury. Financial risks include decisions or activities that may affect your ability to make or keep money. And the third type of risk people worry about taking is psychological risk.

Psychological risk means putting yourself in a situation where you could fail, and you're afraid that people will judge you for it. So you worry. As a sales coach, you can take the people who are worried about taking a risk through a hypothetical situation.

For example, let's say your salesperson has an opportunity to hire a staff person. That's the change she wants to make, but when she thinks about doing it, she starts worrying about the immediate problems that could result. She's not thinking of how a staff person could benefit her, because those benefits are in the future.

So, you can ask her what might happen if she makes the change. She may tell you that she could hire the wrong person, or that it won't work out, or that she's going to have to spend time training the person and that her income will go down. She may say that if she hires the wrong person, she'll have to fire him or her. Then, as her sales coach, you ask her, so what's the worst that could happen if you make the change?

Almost always, the "worst" thing in someone's mind is way worse than what actually happens. With our salesperson, presumably the worst that could happen is that she's going to hire the wrong person, have to fire that person, and get sued for unfair termination. Those things do happen. They are real.

But next you ask, "How likely is that to happen?" Most people then realize that the worst thing that could happen is not very likely to happen. This reduces worry and frees them to think more creatively.

You're not discounting the worst because it can happen, but it helps to explore it if this is a realistic worry. And, it also helps to find out how others in similar situations have handled it. You may ask her, "Out of people you know who have hired staff and it didn't work out, how many of them were sued? How did they deal with it?" The idea is to get your salesperson thinking about what's likely to happen, and what she can do to prevent the worst case scenario. She might decide to have someone else take care of the hiring process, or to train the new staff person. In this case, having a qualified human resource person interview and hire the most qualified applicant will help reduce the chance of being sued, and reduce that worry.

The focus of this exercise is to help the salesperson identify what she has to do to put the worry behind her. Salespeople deal with the issue of worry during every sales call, especially in a closing situation where they present a recommendation that solves the client's problems. If they hear a response like, "I'd like to think about it," they know that the client is thinking about the immediate problems that might happen if she implements the change. When a salesperson learns to address her own worries, she'll be better equipped to help clients who are reluctant to make a decision that benefits the client and the salesperson. (Of course, in a sales situation, we don't call it worry, but rather, "handling objections.")

Feeling and Thinking

The next exercise to help people deal with self-defeating thinking is the Feeling and Thinking exercise, found on page 154. Feelings are real. Two hundred thousand years ago, our ancestors had to worry about all kinds of dangers in their environment, so they had a built-in defense mechanism to help protect them—the "fight or flight" response.

We still have that mechanism in place today. When we sense danger, our feelings kick in, and they can control us. Here's what this looks like in a coaching session. If the salesperson goes into fight or flight mode when you challenge him, he may fight you by saying that his sales goal is unrealistic or complain that you never say anything positive to him. Or he may use a flee response, by agreeing with what you're saying—and then never implement it.

What you need to get across to salespeople is that just because feelings occur automatically doesn't mean they have to control you. We all have a choice in life. We can either respond according to our feelings, meaning that negative feelings will cause us to avoid situations, while positive feelings will spur us to take action. But we have another choice, and it's not that complicated.

When you have a negative feeling, you can employ a three-step process. First, stop and recognize the negative feeling. Second, question the negative thinking that goes with the feeling—in other words, figure out what thinking is causing you to feel this way? And third, come up with the new thinking that produces positive feelings instead.

Salespeople must realize that they have this choice. They can let their feelings control them or they can stop, question their thinking, and create new thinking to help them achieve their goals—without being overwhelmed by those negative feelings.

For example, the single most important thing for job security for salespeople is a system to get new clients. One of the most effective ways to get new clients is to ask for referrals, but new salespeople often find this difficult.

If you ask someone how he feels in this situation, he may say, "I feel nervous. I feel anxious. I feel incompetent. I feel like a beggar." These feelings lead to his negative thinking, which is something like, "I don't want to do this—I don't want people to get upset with me. I don't like this situation." As a result of that negative thinking, the salesperson doesn't take action, and he doesn't ask for the referrals.

To change these negative feelings, you first ask the salesperson how he'd like to feel when he asks for referrals. He may say, "I'd like to feel more confident. I'd like to feel comfortable. I'd like to feel at ease. I'd like to feel competent." We know that thinking can create feelings, so the next question to explore is what positive thinking would make him feel good about this situation?

The salesperson may need to get back to thinking about how he can help people, or a specific goal he has, or how getting more referrals can give him a better quality of life or benefit his family. He may need to think about how serving as a resource to people will help them be more successful. Then you can ask him what beliefs would give him more confidence to embrace this kind of thinking. That belief might be that the people he works with are happy with what he does, and that they've benefited from it.

Remember, this is an example of a normal fear that can be overcome with time. With practice, it will go away. Next, you can explore this question with the salesperson—"As a result of wanting to feel better and having thinking that produces more positive feelings and beliefs, what are you going to do differently?"

The answer might be that the salesperson decides to develop some language to ask for referrals that he feels comfortable with. Maybe he's been trained on something specific to say, but realizes that different language he's heard other salespeople use feels like a better fit for him. The point is that with this exercise, you want to show the salesperson how negative feelings create negative thinking, and then turn it around to show how he thinks can change his feelings for the better.

Change and Loss

The next exercise, found on page 155, you can use addresses change and loss. Sales coaches sometimes underestimate the negative impact of change or loss, but a salesperson who is struggling to make a major change or who loses a big sale can go into a big funk for a long period of time. This takes energy away from making progress, so whenever a salesperson is implementing significant change or experiences a loss, you should take them through this exercise, which is designed to help put this change and loss behind them.

When you lose a loved one, you go through a grieving process. This exercise takes the salesperson through a similar process. You need to get her talking about the negative aspects of the change or loss because even if you manage to put a positive spin on the loss, it still has negative consequences for her. Let's use an example of a salesperson who didn't get the promotion she'd been hoping for, which would have given her a better territory with a stronger market opportunity to help accelerate her career growth. Unfortunately, she wasn't the best candidate for this promotion, and she didn't get it.

She's tremendously disappointed, and you can't just say, "Get over it." It's not that simple. This is a huge loss for her. Loss can send people into a state of depression where they have no energy, and stop working and being as productive as they could be. Worse yet, they may not even be aware of this because they are so disappointed.

As the person's sales coach, you need to take her through a series of questions and talk about what she's thinking and feeling. You need to make her aware that you understand there are negative aspects to this change or loss, and show empathy for her situation before you can encourage her to deal with the reality of the situation. In other words, you've got to get all the bad stuff out on the table before you can help her turn the situation around.

She might say something like, "This is going to cause me to take longer to achieve my goals, or this is going to disappoint my family because I've already talked about what we were going to be able to do if I got this promotion." This loss may affect her immediately—she may not be able to buy something she'd planned to buy—and she may also be worried about what her peers will think.

After you've explored these aspects with her, you can ask, "How would you like things to be?" If she says she'd like things to be different, and that she'd like to get the promotion right away, you can ask, "How likely are those things going to happen immediately?" That's when reality kicks in for her. The answer is not likely. When she realizes that lamenting what she didn't get isn't going to do anything, she becomes responsible for adapting to it.

To drive this point home, you might ask a question like, "How long will it take you to accept the reality of the loss?" She might say it will take a long time, or that she may be able to get over it fairly quickly. The more important question to ask is, "What are the consequences if you can't accept the change?"

You want her to realize that the consequences are negative. She might say, "Well, if I don't accept this change, I'm going to continue to be mad. I'm going to continue to throw a pity party for myself. I'm not going to work as hard, and that really hurts me, not the company."

To help her move forward with the change or loss, ask what has the change caused her to think about that wouldn't have happened without this experience? She may have to accept the reality that she didn't implement the new learning she needed, or that she wasn't as proactive as she could be to accelerate the growth of her own career. She may admit that the loss or change made her realize that she's responsible for her career success, or that she needs to take her career growth more seriously.

Of course, some people have a hard time getting around to saying this. This process might take several meetings over a period of time, but one of the biggest things about accepting change and loss is forgiveness. If a higher-up didn't promote you or didn't give you the territory you wanted, you may have to forgive that person to move on. The phrase I use is: "Lack of forgiveness is like taking poison and hoping the other person dies." If you can forgive people who have negatively impacted your life and realize that they weren't out to punish you, that they just did what they had to, you can get on with your life. Otherwise, you run the risk of staying stuck in the past and clinging to grievances that negatively impact your life.

That's why you explore what the salesperson needs to do to put the change or loss behind her. Realize that the bigger the change or loss experienced, the more difficult it may be or the more time it may take for her to work through this process. Either way, you want to make sure the salesperson understands that the benefits of taking positive action are a much better quality of life than being stuck in the past.

Self-Concept

The final exercise, found on page 151, deals with self-concept. Self-concept can be defined as, "Do I really see myself achieving the goal that I have set for myself?" Again, you have a series of questions to help the person realize that he's done things throughout his life that, at one time, wouldn't have seemed possible. But over time, he figured out a way to achieve them. That's the message you want him to realize.

I'm in a career right now where I help people achieve their goals faster than they could on their own. The idea of this career first entered my mind as a senior in high school. For the final speech in our speech class, our teacher told us we could speak about anything, but suggested that we might want to give a speech on what we'd do with our lives after we graduated. She said that if someone gave a particularly stimulating speech, he or she could give the commencement address for senior graduation.

When I heard her say that, I thought I'd like to do that. I'd like to give the final speech at senior commencement on what we're going to do with the rest of our lives now that we have completed high school. Unfortunately, my self-concept didn't allow me to take action on this. I saw myself as only an average performer. I doubted that anyone would want to listen to me, so I got scared and I changed the topic of my final speech. The speech teacher told me afterward that she was disappointed—that she'd thought I was "much better than this" and that she'd expected me to give a completely different speech. Even though I got an A on my speech, it wasn't the one I really wanted to give because I was too afraid to do it. My self-concept wouldn't let me.

However, I eventually did give a speech to the senior class at the high school I graduated from about how to make progress on goals that you set for yourself—but it was twenty years after I graduated. Even though it took me a long time to achieve a goal that I originally established, I was able to do it because my self-concept had changed. It had changed because of things that I'd learned and life experiences that gave me more confidence in what I was doing.

The Self-Concept Exercise and the questions that go with it are designed to get salespeople to see that they have accomplished things in their lives that they may have once thought were impossible—and that they can do this again. One is, "What things have you accomplished that at one time you thought were never possible?" We've all done things similar to the story I just shared. Another question is, "What goals do you want to accomplish but don't know how?"

There are other questions in the Self-Concept Exercise to explore with salespeople. One of them is, "If you didn't need other people's approval, what would you want to achieve?" It's all too easy to let other people's approval get in the way of what we want to accomplish.

The purpose of this exercise is to get salespeople to realize that anything is possible. They might not be great (yet), but they can always get better. Then you can ask, what do you think you are going to do next? As a coach, your most critical role is helping salespeople change or improve their self-concept when their self-concept is preventing them from reaching their goals. If you only teach the people you work with one thing, it might be this—that self-concept can be changed.

Your Goal as a Coach: Helping Salespeople Change

I know this firsthand. Over time, my self-concept has changed for the better. Why? Because of the coaches I've worked with. I've had coaches I respected who challenged me to do things I didn't think I was capable of to create drive. I had coaches who were great teachers. And I was fortunate to have a great psychiatrist who helped me realize that I'd drawn faulty conclusions about past events that had made me doubt my capabilities. Even today, I have people in my life who challenge me to do things I didn't think were possible.

The coaches who have helped me change had great playbooks. They knew a variety of strategies to create drive, to encourage new learning, and to overcome self-defeating thinking. They helped me set and achieve new goals. This book is an example of one of those goals. I'd had the idea for this book for a decade, and finally it's come to fruition.

While writing a book and seeing how people would respond creates anxiety, I had to stop worrying about what people would think about the book and focus on the fact that I wanted to do it. I wrote it because I wanted to make an impact on people's lives. I've already done workshops with the content of this book, and I know it makes a difference for both sales coaches and the people they work with. This book will make a difference for you as well.

At the beginning, I explained how this book is designed to be your play-book when you're working with salespeople of all levels of experience and ability. It's not designed just for superstars—after all, the superstars will take care of themselves. This book gives you a system and specific strategies to use to help salespeople change, which in turn impacts their careers and their personal lives as well.

The saying, "People change but seldom" is bogus. People do change. But it doesn't happen overnight, and it's hard for people to make change on their own. That's where you come in. As a sales coach, you can help salespeople change—and change more quickly, more dramatically, and more exten-sively—than they could on their own. You'll find that you change in the process as well.

As a coach, that's what I hope the content of this book can help you do—to change both your own self-concept, and that of the people you work with over time. Whether you're playing the role of a motivator, a teacher or a shrink, the concepts and exercises will help you be a more effective coach, and make a positive impact in the lives of the people you touch. That's the true purpose—and the true payoff—of being a coach.

Appendix

The following table is a summary of when to use each of the documents included in this Appendix.

Document	Page	Purpose
Growth Rate	126	A sales leader or salesperson uses this to assess which areas need to be addressed to accelerate growth.
Vision	127	A sales leader uses this as a template to create their vision.
Values	128	A process to determine the values of a salesperson to see if they fit in with the organization.
Balanced Goals	130	An exercise to determine if a salesperson has a goal of wanting a much better quality of life than they currently have.
Behavioral Traits	132	A series of questions to find out if the salesperson has the traits necessary to be more successful in their career.
Focus Document	142	The template for developing a one-page business plan.
Breakthrough Learning Document	143	The template for developing a tactical plan to implement the key strategy and overcome, if any, self-defeating thinking.
Feelings	147	When a salesperson has difficulty expressing feelings and communicating at level four of the relationship, use this document and have them select the feelings they are experiencing so you can understand the emotional problem.
Personal Frustration	148	A series of questions to ask a person you are coaching when you start sensing tension in the relationship.
Coaching Review	149	The agenda for a one-on-one coaching session. The salesperson completes this document prior to the meeting.

Document	Page	Purpose
Drive	150	A series of questions to ask a salesperson when their drive score is low.
Self-Concept	151	If the salesperson has difficulty seeing themselves achieving at a higher level, ask these questions.
Resistance to Change	152	Use with a salesperson who is in stability or success stage of their career and who is struggling with making a change they know will help them be more successful.
Worry	153	Use this with anyone who is fearful of making a change because they think something bad will happen.
Feeling and Thinking	154	When a salesperson lets their negative feelings control their behavior, use this series of questions.
Change and Loss	155	If a salesperson is anticipating or dealing with change they don't like, use this series of questions to assist them in accepting the reality of the change. Use also to help the person deal with disappointment or lost sales.

Blank versions of the documents listed above may be downloaded from the author's Web site at: www.bobteichart.com

Growth Rate

What is the Goal?

_____

When, in your professional life, were you the most driven? If that time is a 10, what is your drive now on a scale of 1 to 10 in relation to the goal? Put the answer above the D below.

Consider individuals who have already achieved the career results you want on a consistent basis and give them a 10 rating. How much new learning do you need to get where they are, with 1 being a lot and 10 is none. Put your answer above the NL below.

Think about the most positive, upbeat person you know who takes risks, gets over disappointment easily, and seems to initiate change quickly, and give him or her a 1 for self-defeating thinking. What is your level of self-defeating thinking on a scale of 1 to 10, with 10 being extreme self-defeating thinking and 1 being no self-defeating thinking? Put your answer above the SDT below, and then complete the equation to determine your rate of growth.

Your Growth Rate

$$\underline{\qquad} + \underline{\qquad} - 2(\underline{\qquad}) = \underline{\qquad}$$
$$D + NL - 2(SDT) = Growth\ Rate$$

Maximum score is an 18. The higher the score, the faster you will get to the goal.

What are your thoughts after doing this exercise?

Vision

IMPACT — *Why I am in business*

CORE VALUES — *How I will conduct business*

EXCEPTIONAL GOAL — *What I want to accomplish*

VIVID DESCRIPTION — *What I will see happening*

Values

List six decisions you have made during your life.

1.

2.

3.

4.

5.

6.

Look at the list of values on the next page. Under each decision above, list the values that were part of the decision-making process. Then answer these questions.

What are your thoughts about this exercise?

What are your core values?

How does knowing your values both help and hinder change and growth?

How can you use what you learned in the future?

Accountability	Learn
Aggression	Lifestyle
Assertiveness	Love
Beauty	Management
Build	Mastery
Challenge	Open communication
Control	Political concerns
Competence	Recognition
Complexity	Religion
Cooperation	Security
Country	Simplicity
Courage	Service
Creativity	Social responsibility
Entrepreneurship	Structure
Explore	Success
Family	Teamwork
Fitness	Trust
Flexibility	Wealth
Freedom	
Fun	
Growth	
Happiness	
Health	
Honesty	
Independence	
Integrity	

Balanced Goals

In each of the six areas, list the goals you want to achieve in the next 3–5 years.

Education   What I want to learn just for the sake of learning or the learning that might help me in the other five areas.

Family   What are things I want to do with my family? What are the things I want for my family?

Career and Financial   What accomplishments do I want to achieve? What are my key financial goals?

Health and Fitness   What are things I want to do related to sports? What are general health goals I have?

Social and Cultural   What are the things I want to do just for fun?

Spiritual   What do I want to do to have a sense of inner peace?

Out of all the three- to five-year goals listed on the previous page, which three are most important? List them below and put down your reasons as to why they are important.

Goals	Reason for Importance

Now that you have listed your goals, go back and put a dollar amount next to each goal that will cost money.

What will your adjusted gross income need to be to pay for the goals listed and pay your current bills?

Adjusted Gross Income Needed _____

Behavioral Traits

INTERVIEW QUESTIONS

Ask the candidate the three questions for each behavioral trait. Based on the answers, give the candidate a rating of how well they possess that trait, where 1 is low and 10 is high. At the end of the interview, add the ten ratings together. The higher the score, the more likely the candidate is to have a successful career in sales.

BEHAVIORAL TRAIT: *Motivation and Work Ethic*

1. *Tell me about a time when you were able to provide your own motivation, even though you were working alone.*

_____

_____

2. *Tell me about a goal you achieved that required long hours over a long period of time.*

_____

_____

3. *Tell me about a time in your life when you lacked motivation.*

_____

_____

Rating 1–10 _____

continued on next page

BEHAVIORAL TRAIT: *Building Relationships*

1. *Give me an example of your ability to build a relationship with a difficult individual.*

   _____

   _____

2. *How have you demonstrated your concern for another person when you had other priorities?*

   _____

   _____

3. *Tell me about a situation where you weren't able to build a relationship with someone with whom you did want to have a relationship.*

   _____

   _____

Rating 1–10 _____

continued on next page

BEHAVIORAL TRAIT: *Ability to Influence*

1. When have you been able to influence the behavior of a person who initially wanted to do something else?

   _____

   _____

2. How have you gone about getting a person to follow your lead?

   _____

   _____

3. Tell me about a time when you weren't able to influence someone.

   _____

   _____

Rating 1–10 _____

continued on next page

BEHAVIORAL TRAIT: *Assertiveness*

1. *Tell me about a time when you had to be assertive in giving directions to others.*

   _____

   _____

2. *When have you had to challenge the opinion of someone with more authority or status than you?*

   _____

   _____

3. *Tell me about a time when you weren't assertive and the situation turned out badly.*

   _____

   _____

Rating 1–10 _____

continued on next page

BEHAVIORAL TRAIT: *Awareness*

1.   Give me an example of how your intuition helped you uncover the real concerns of the person you were speaking to.

_____

_____

2.   When have you been able to understand another person's point of view that was different from yours?

_____

_____

3.   Tell me about a time when you weren't perceptive of the needs of others.

_____

_____

Rating 1–10 _____

continued on next page

BEHAVIORAL TRAIT: *Problem-Solving*

1. *Tell me about the most difficult task you have had to learn on your own.*

_____

_____

2. *What is a difficult problem you have had to solve while working in a group with others? How did you go about solving the problem?*

_____

_____

3. *Tell me about a time when you let your emotions get in the way of problem-solving.*

_____

_____

Rating 1–10 _____

continued on next page

BEHAVIORAL TRAIT: *Creating Energy*

1. Tell me about a time when you were able to motivate others. How did you do it?

_____

_____

2. When were you able to create your own energy to accomplish something you wanted?

_____

_____

3. Tell me about a time when you weren't able to motivate others. What was going on?

_____

_____

Rating 1–10 _____

continued on next page

BEHAVIORIAL TRAIT: *Goal-Setting*

1. *What is your current system of goal-setting?*

_____

_____

2. *What is the goal you are most proud of achieving? How long did it take to achieve and how did you do it?*

_____

_____

3. *Tell me about a time when goals weren't important.*

_____

_____

Rating 1–10 _____

continued on next page

BEHAVIORAL TRAIT: *Coping*

1. *Tell me about a major disappointment you have encountered and how you have dealt with it.*

_____

_____

2. *Tell me about a difficult personal rejection you have had to deal with.*

_____

_____

3. *When have you not been able to handle personal disappointment well?*

_____

_____

Rating 1–10 _____

continued on next page

BEHAVIORAL TRAIT: *Decision-Making*

1. *Tell me about a difficult decision you have made with limited input from others.*

_____

_____

2. *When have you had to make an unpopular decision? What happened?*

_____

_____

3. *Tell me about a decision you made that didn't turn out well.*

_____

_____

Rating 1–10 _____

TOTAL RATING 10–100 _____

This is total score of the ten behavioral traits.

Focus Document

PURPOSE — *What I do for others*

VALUE — *What separates me from other salespeople*

PAYOFF — *What I get as a result of achieving my purpose*

NEEDS — *What I don't have enough of*

KEY GOALS — *What I must achieve that will give me what I need*

KEY STRATEGIES — *How I will achieve my goals*

SUPPORT — *What I need from others so I can perform at my best*

Breakthrough Learning Document

FOCUS: _____ to _____

KEY STRATEGY OUTCOME

Pick one of the key strategies from the Focus Document.

What would be the expected results after three months of working on the key strategy?

POSITIVE REWARDS

What are the positive rewards for implementing the breakthrough?

NEGATIVE CONSEQUENCES

What are the negative consequences if the breakthrough isn't implemented?

continued on next page

SELF-DEFEATING THINKING

What will you need to stop doing or find a better way of doing to find time for implementing the breakthrough?

What new problems might you encounter as you implement the breakthrough?

What feelings do you have when thinking about implementing the breakthrough?

What belief might prevent implementation of the breakthrough?

continued on next page

TACTICS

What will I do differently to implement the breakthrough and minimize self-defeating thinking?

Consider:

Skills: Knowledge:

Habits: Staff:

Marketing Procedures: Operational Procedures:

Technology Usage: Financial Issues:

New Beliefs: New Thinking:

continued on next page

SCORE CARD

What are the key measurements to review monthly that indicate your business is growing?

Feelings

joy
happy
bummed
bored
lonely
angry
mad
discouraged
frustrated
imitated
appreciated
wistful
gypped
ripped off
proud
inadequate
unloved
grateful
excited
agitated
nervous
dumb
annoyed
hopeful
uncertain
ecstatic
ashamed
guilty
embarrassed
tense
uptight
comfortable
puzzled
confused
disgusted
revolted

self-conscious
ornery
resentful
naughty
crabby
pressured
afraid
scared
silly
frightened
intimidated
envious
jealous
melancholy
hate
dislike
loved
liked
sexy
disinterested
playful
regretful
left out
rejected
hurt
stumped
lost
enthusiastic
empty
accepting
understood
infuriated
carefree
disheartened
childish
anticipation

righteous
indignant
uncomfortable
anxious
burdened
cornered
getting even
revengeful
competent
abused
distrustful
trusting
defeated
recognized
important
satisfied
criticized
dissatisfied
support
energetic
fed-up
bugged
persistent
stubborn
respect
judged
disappointed
glad
sad
pretty
witty
gay
odd
taken aback
surprised
startled

Personal Frustration

1. *I'm having a difficult time being a resource to you in your career. Do you feel the same way? What can we do about it?*

2. *What is getting in the way of my helping you solve your problems?*

3. *I really don't know you. Can you tell me more about yourself?*

4. *To be a resource, I need to know more about your fears, anxieties, and frustrations.*

5. *What do I need to do to earn the right to be more of a resource?*

6. *Who else have you had a difficult relationship with?*

7. *I feel like we are fighting a battle. Do you feel the same way? What can we do about it?*

Coaching Review

Continued growth is the result of drive and new learning minus the interference of self-defeating thinking that clutters the mind.

1. *What is going well?*

2. *What do you want to talk about?*

3. *Rate your progress on your breakthrough on a scale of 1 to 7.*
    (1 is poor, 7 is exceptional)

4. *What needs to be done to improve rating?*

Consider:

    Drive — Look at your purpose, values, support, rewards, and negative consequences.

    New learning — Look at your skills, knowledge, and other tactics.

    Self-defeating thinking — Look at beliefs, new problems, negative feelings, and rewarding activities that might need to be given up.

5. *Review Score Card.*

6. *Commitments from last meeting and results.*

7. *On a scale of 1–7, with 1 being low, how helpful was this session? What would make it better?*

Drive

1. What goal has created drive, energy and motivation in the past?

2. What were the reasons this goal was important?

3. What need did it satisfy?

4. What were the reasons the need was so important?

5. From whom were you looking for approval?

6. Did you get the approval you wanted?

7. What helped you stay focused on the goal?

8. What did people say to you as you were making progress on the goal?

9. Did you ask others for help?

Self-Concept

1. *What things have you accomplished that at one time you never thought were possible?*

2. *What things have you achieved that, as you look back, you wonder how you ever did them?*

3. *What are goals you want to accomplish but don't know how?*

4. *What goals have you achieved that at first you didn't know how you were going to accomplish them?*

5. *What got you to start learning how to achieve those goals?*

6. *If you knew you couldn't fail, what would you want to accomplish?*

7. *If you didn't need other people's approval, what would you want to achieve?*

8. *What are you thinking after answering these questions?*

9. *What are you going to do next?*

10. *Do you need any support?*

Resistance to Change

List the change you want to make.

Answer these questions:

1. *What are you afraid might happen if you made the change?*

2. *What would you have to give up in each area?*

   a. Ego/Identity
   b. Relationships
   c. Rewarding Activities

3. *How will the change impact others?*

4. *Is there a conflict between this change and your values or beliefs?*

5. *What are your feelings when you think about implementing the change?*

6. *What is your plan to minimize the resistance and make the change?*

Worry

1. What change do you want to make?

2. What do you think might happen if you made the change?

3. What is the worst thing that could happen to you if you made the change?

4. How likely is that to happen?

5. What is the worst that has happened to others in this situation? How often did it happen? How did they deal with it?

6. What is likely to happen based on your experience and the experience of others? How would you respond?

7. If the worst did happen, then what would you do?

8. Based on this discussion, what do you need to do to put this worry behind you?

Feeling and Thinking

1. *What situation is difficult for you to deal with?*

2. *How do you feel when in the situation listed?*

3. *What is your negative thinking when you have these negative feelings?*

4. *How do you act as a result of your negative thinking and feelings?*

5. *How would you like to feel?*

6. *What positive thinking would help you feel better about the situation?*

7. *What beliefs would give you more confidence?*

8. *As a result of your positive thinking and beliefs, what will you do?*

Change and Loss

The following are a series of questions to assist individuals in handling and working through any change, loss, or major disappointment.

1. *What are you thinking related to the change/loss?*

2. *What are the negative aspects of the change/loss?*

3. *How will the change impact you immediately?*

4. *How would you like things to be?*

5. *How likely is it that those things will happen?*

6. *How long will it take you to accept the reality of the change?*

7. *What are the consequences if you can't accept the change?*

8. *What has this change made you to think about that would not have happened if you had not had this experience?*

9. *Whom do you need to forgive?*

10. *What is the future like without forgiveness?*

11. *Based on our conversation, what is a positive step you can take to put this change/loss behind you?*

12. *What are the payoffs for taking this positive action?*